I0771277

LETTERS
TO SHIRLEY

1st Lieut. P. M. Potts Jr.
c/o Commando d'Aeronautica a disposizione
Zona di Guerra, Italia.
American Exp. F.

Officer's
Mail

Mrs. Paul M. Potts, Jr.
Natchitoches
Louisiana   U. S.
Stat

O.K. Paul M. Potts Jr.
1st Lieut. A. S. Sig. R. C.

Letters to Shirley

LETTERS HOME FROM AN
AMERICAN WORLD WAR I AVIATOR

COMPILED AND EDITED BY

Marion Potts Clayton

PARKE PRESS
Norfolk, Virginia

DEDICATION

*To my husband, Howard Clayton, for his vision
and constant encouragement. He never knew my father but
the most touching thing he said after reading the letters was,
"I would have liked this man had I known him."
Most people did.*

and

*To my mother, Shirley Sawyer Potts,
for the safe keeping of these letters and
giving them to me.*

LETTERS TO SHIRLEY
Copyright © 2012 Marion Potts Clayton

All rights reserved. Published in the United States by Parke Press, Norfolk, VA

*No part of this book may be reproduced in any manner whatsoever
without written permission, except in the case of brief quotations
used for the purpose of critical articles and reviews.*

Library of Congress Control Number is available upon request.
ISBN 978-0-9843339-7-4

Published by Parke Press, Norfolk, Virginia • www.parkepress.com

DESIGNED BY MARSHALL ROUSE MCCLURE

Manufactured in the United States of America

TABLE OF CONTENTS

PREFACE

I WAS BORN in Natchitoches, Louisiana in 1928, almost 11 years after the last letter in this collection was written. The father I knew as I grew up was the man who erected a platform in our yard and put a tripod on it, and then carried his telescope up so he could better study the constellations. He also built a boat, and a house down on the farm for my grandmother, "Mother Rollins" of the letters. My father had many special interests including Louisiana history, Louisiana crops and swamps, Indian lore, and the Ozark Mountains up in Arkansas – where he insisted we should go camping from time to time. I did not know that my father had been a flyer, though I had noticed him watch with great interest the crop dusters do their aerobatics in the air above his cotton crop.

When I was young, World War I was already ancient history – it was in the past. However, I was aware of World War II because my brothers-in-law were in the service and overseas. My parents, Paul and Shirley Potts, turned the radio on to hear the war news many times every day. We had army maneuvers all over Louisiana, and certainly my town of Natchitoches was swarming with servicemen and military trucks. But I was young, and my youthful thoughts all revolved around myself and my young friends in high school.

I grew up. My father had died and I had moved to Virginia. Visiting me, my mother handed me a box of letters. She said, "These are letters from Paul. I want you to have them." The letters were bundled, bound by a faded pink ribbon and tucked in a box of nearly the same age as the letters. I thought they were old love letters and, therefore, private. So they stayed in the box, still bound by the pink ribbon, unread for 40 years.

I'm grateful to my husband, Howard, who made me read these letters after I held onto them for 40 years. I always wondered why my mother chose me, the youngest, to keep my father's letters, and I hope she would approve of my attempts at their preservation and publication. The family home burned, but these letters and pictures luckily – miraculously – survived.

After reading my father's letters, I became very interested in many aspects of "The Great War" and the air service in which he was a commissioned Lieutenant. For instance, I wanted to know more about the Caproni airplane. From reading the letters, I thought my father seemed especially fond of the Caproni because of the way it handled. I think I gasped when he wrote "Gee, I felt funny!" He was telling of the many hours he spent flying a different kind of plane, only to find out it had just been removed from service and condemned!

Another example of my new interest in aviation: I read an article about the June 1, 2009, fatal Air France flight from Rio de Janeiro to Paris. The article was headlined "Deadly plunge at 38,000 feet." The report stated that the co-pilot continued to bring the nose up, but still plunged 10,000 feet per minute, crashing in 3½ minutes into the Atlantic Ocean and killing all on board. Later, as I transcribed the letter I named "Three Stalks of Wheat or Not at 200 Meters," I read my father's explanation that you nose *down* to keep from stalling, but not as low as 200 meters (because you will drop at least that far before you can straighten out and gain speed). My father described how pulling the nose up will exacerbate an aerodynamic stall. The information I had read about the Air France crash resonated as I read his letter: My dad knew about this very phenomenon at age 22, in the earliest days of learning to fly, almost a hundred years ago.

WHEN I DECIDED TO PUBLISH my father's letters, my husband and I felt that they could make a significant contribution as "source material," so, for authenticity's sake, they are printed *as written.* (Because I know my father was a literate, well-educated man, it grieved me to include mistakes, such as fragmented sentences, and *don't* and *won't* punctuated inconsistently. But Paul Potts wrote these letters just for his wife, and he certainly did not intend them to be published. Otherwise, I'm sure he would have been more attentive to his grammar.)

I created titles for each of these "stories" to keep them straight as I transcribed them, and in some cases added a little comment that follows the title directly. Otherwise, every word is part of the letters beginning with the return address and ending with the censor's "OK."

ALL THE ORIGINAL LETTERS have been preserved in acid-free sleeves and archival boxes, but for the purpose of publishing I transcribed them. It was quite a push for me to type these many letters, and I hope those of you who read them will have an appreciation for Paul's service and my efforts in reproducing them. As for publication, I have to thank Marshall McClure for her interest, guidance and special talents. She has been a pleasure to work with and I have great respect for her professionalism.

Marion Potts Clayton

The editor, around 1932, in Natchitoches, Louisiana

INTRODUCTION

PAUL MIMMS POTTS, JR. grew up in Natchitoches (pronounced *Nak-a-tish*), Louisiana. This little college town is known as the oldest town in the Louisiana Purchase, with its main street laid in bricks, running along the Cane River, with French verandas on the storefronts.

Paul was the third child of Paul Mimms Potts, Sr., who at the time of World War I had several enterprises, one of which was cotton farming. Paul, Jr.'s older brother, Robert, was a doctor in New Orleans; his sister, Lillian, was married and lived in Texas; and his younger brother, William (Billie), lived at home.

Young Paul enrolled in VMI in 1913. By May of 1917 he had left VMI to volunteer for the U.S. Army. But he was instead selected for the U.S. Air Service, a very new and young service, and was sent to Kelley Field in Texas for training. Shortly afterward, he traveled to New York to board a Europe-bound troop ship as part of the American Expeditionary Force, leaving his brand-new wife, Shirley, with his parents in their Natchitoches home. Shirley was pregnant at age 21, the only child of Belle Baird Rollins who is referred to in Paul's letters as "Mother Rollins."

These letters Paul wrote to his young wife during his time in Europe are full of love and longing, the universal substance of soldiers' letters home. But additionally, the letters contain detailed descriptions of the education and development of this young aviator, a narrative which parallels the rapidly evolving aviation experiment of the U.S. Army.

All the airmen's letters had to be carefully censored. In fact, one letter from Paul was censored and signed by Fiorello La Guardia (or his agent) who, according to Shirley Potts, was the young Italian captain of Potts's Italian Squadriglia. The man who became mayor of New York city in fact did go to France to select American flyers for the Italian training schools, so it is probable that he is the same man.*

A note to readers: It is important to try to grasp just how rudimentary the elements of an airplane were in that day. It had to have an engine for power, wings for lift, propeller for thrust, and simple movable parts including a rudder and ailerons. The pilot and co-pilot sat in an open cockpit exposed to rain and cold temperatures and flew at anywhere from 3,000 to 12,000 feet. The plane shook so much it felt like it might come apart. It had no brakes. Imagine cutting the motor in order to slow your speed to prepare for a landing! Potts is said to have mentioned that pilots crave speed in the air because speed is what keeps the plane up. This unattributed quote sums it up: "Thou must maintain thine airspeed lest the Earth rise up and smite thee." And, can you imagine what the runway was like, especially at night with only torches lit to show where to land? Paul Potts' letters tell how nerve-wracking it was to fly at night, sometimes carrying bombs to the enemy.

WHEN THE GREAT WAR was over, Paul Potts returned to his "Babykinses": his wife, Shirley, and new baby daughter, Pauline (who later dropped "Pauline" for "Paula."). They stayed in Natchitoches and had three other children. Potts remained faithful to his principles, was respected in his community, and remained devoted to Shirley. They had been married for 36 years when he died in 1953.

* See Notes, page 256.

PAUL'S FAMILY
and Flying Friends in Europe

§

Lt. Paul M. Potts, Jr. – A Natchitoches, Louisiana twenty-two year old; a Virginia Military Institute (VMI) cadet, (1913-1917) volunteering in the U.S. Army, selected for the American Air Service; author of 78 letters to his bride, Shirley, while serving as an aviator in World War I.

Shirley Sawyer Potts – Paul's twenty-one year old Louisiana bride of less than 4 months; educated at Dominican College in New Orleans, Louisiana; living with Paul's family in Natchitoches; expecting their first child in April and awaiting Paul's return from the war.

Pauline – The first child of Paul and Shirley, born April 16, 1918 in Natchitoches while Paul was training in Italy.

Mother Rollins – Belle Baird Rollins, Shirley's mother and mother-in-law of Paul.

Papa – Paul Mimms Potts, Sr., cotton planter in Natchitoches, Louisiana, father of Paul; also father of oldest son, Robert, only daughter, Lillian and youngest son, William.

Robert – Older brother of Paul, a medical doctor practicing in New Orleans, Louisiana; married to Margaret.

Lillian – Older sister of Paul, ("Sis"), living in Texas; lively, energetic and frequent visitor home with her own child.

Will – Paul's younger brother ("Billie"), living at home in Natchitoches; very attentive to Shirley and devoted to Paul (lends him $25 to go to war).

Some WWI buddies and fliers – Curt Keen, West Texas; Dug Farquhar, Maryland; Norman Sweetser, New England; Spence Hart, Virginia; John Ross, Macon, Georgia; Sam Long, Tupelo, Mississippi; Ed Smith, Mississippi; Earl Forsythe; McCain; Coupland; Earnest Whittemore; Walter (?), Letzig; Griffin; Mason (killed); Stone and Adriance (both had serious crashes); and Fiorello LaGuardia, New York.

Billie Potts at the "Green House" in Natchitoches, La.

Paul Mimms Potts, Jr. during his time at
Virginia Military Institute

Shirley Sawyer Potts

LETTERS
to SHIRLEY

❦ ARRIVAL IN LIVERPOOL ❧

Oct. 1st, 1917

My own precious darling baby –

I've made the trip across O.K. and now I'm going to write you a little love note and send it back on the ship I came on. I can't put all the love I want to in the letters the censor's read but later darling I guess I'll have to regardless of the censor for I can't go very long without telling my baby a little of how I love and worship her. Sweetest most precious girl in the whole world.

OCTOBER 1, 1917

Darling this delay looks bad for my early return home but dont you worry a bit about it honey for I'm sure it will all work out alright and although I'll be a month later getting back to you, at least, I'll get back to you in plenty of time for that wonderful thing that is to happen. I will be with my little girl through your ordeal if I have to swim the Atlantic.

Darling I'm so afraid you wont take care of your precious

self like you should when I'm not there to look after you. You mustn't forget darling what you mean to me and that you must go through with everything without anything happening to you. If you let anything happen to yourself darling you will be ruining your husband for I cannot get along now without my baby wife. Mother will or should know how you should take care of yourself if you let her know you need advice. You sweet thing, there's nothing to it, you should have your husband to look after you now. But darling when I get back from France you are going to have me to look after you from then on. For I wont be separated from you again.

Listen honey – you must try to tell me how you are getting on for if I don't know honey I'll be worrying myself to death. Tell me all new developments darling for I must know. I just think you are going to be the most wonderful precious little mother in this wide world. I'm getting jealous of my own baby already because it will have you for "mother" while I can only have you for "wife". But when I come back I'm going to claim my share of you. Think there will be anything left of you then, darling?

When I get to my flying school darling I will probably learn definitely what I have in the future to look forward to. That is the time it will take me to complete my training, when I will get my commission and when I will get back. If the censor doesn't cut it out I'll of course write you all my plans so you will know what to look forward to with me. We go ashore in Liverpool tomorrow and go by train to London. How long we will be in London I don't know. I don't think it will be over a week at most. I hope not precious. I understand I'm to be paid regularly over here sweetheart and of course as I need very little myself now since I have all my outfit that I had to buy I'm going to see what the chances are of getting the rest back to you at periods of about every two months. If you don't need it then it will be well saved. If you need money at any time darling you must tell me, hear? And I'll see that you get it. Hear now, my precious darling wonderful little wife. I love you. I just worship you and you don't know darling girl what a difference it makes now in my happiness since you are my own precious wife. Mine forever.

Be sure and tell Sister and Bob & M. that I made it over O.K. and give a little of my love to Mama Papa and Will and take the rest for your own sweet self. My two babies. With a million long long long soul kisses and hard tight close hugs and all my love.

Your Own Devoted Husband

If I find I can send you money alright I'm going to send Will $25 that I owe him and Dad his when "Sam" pays me off enough. Be a good little wife and get fat and stay good looking.

§ TOY TRAIN ཇ

Paul travels by train as Europe is engaged in a war on two fronts – the Eastern Front and the Western Front.

Oct. 17th 1917
Italy

Dearest Babykins –

Haven't received any letter from you since I got down here but really don't suppose it has had time to be sent down from Paris. You know I have received two letters from you since I came over.

Now since I'm settled I can tell you what I've been doing. After I landed I lost no time to speak of in getting to Paris. The trip down from the seaport to Paris was very interesting to me.

OCTOBER 17, 1917

The country was wonderful. Almost a solid garden all the way, and so many little old stone houses with thatched roofs and picturesque towns. The railroad was very amusing to me. It was like a toy railroad. Little cars that look like a man could push them as fast as the little tin engine pulled them. By the way at most of the stations the "baggage men" were ladies.

Upon my arrival in Paris I put up at the D'Albany Hotel which is recommended to Americans because the desk clerk and head waiter speak a little English. However the rest of the hotel personnel spoke no word of English until I left when I had the elevator boy saying "going up or going down". In Paris there were two days a week when we couldn't have meat to eat and could only have a warm bath or warm water of any description on Saturdays and Sundays because coal is very scarce.

By means of an English-French dictionary I was able to "Parle vous" enough "Francois" to get along quite well.

I was in Paris a whole week and the only thing that kept me from being absolutely happy was that you were not with me to help me enjoy it all, you sweet little girl. It is absolutely a wonderful place. Everything seems to be put there only with the idea of beauty. No ugly buildings and streets like our cities. I visited "Les Invalides" where Napoleon is buried but didn't get to see his tomb because it was locked up. But it was a very old place with the most beautiful grounds, a palace fit for any king to be buried in. I also walked along the Champs-Elysees, the Place de Concorde and wandered through the Teuilleries (*sic*) Gardens and it was great. By the way my hotel was on the Rue de Rivoli which is written about so often in novels. The last day I was there I went through the Louvre, that is the part now open and took a long walk down the Seine along which there are hundreds of ancient book stalls full of musty old volumes of every character and description. I know you have read of them. I ended the day about 5 o'clock when I came to the Notre Dame Cathedral which is on a large island in the Seine. It was truly a wonderful "little church". It was beautiful from the outside, looking so ancient, grand and peaceful. I went inside and dropped a franc in the silver tray by the huge doors and I guess thousands of other sightseers have dropped thousands of other francs in the same tray. I walked around the outside of a big dome in the center and it was like an art gallery. Only of course there were little rooms and places to kneel in prayer all the way around. Before I left I went into the center which is the church part proper and has a wonderful pulpit and is so vast and large it makes you feel like a pygmy. There were numbers of people praying there then so I said a prayer too. I felt real blue because you weren't there to go through it with me. I know how you would have enjoyed it. If I had been there one more day I was going to go out to Versailles, the place where the old kings lived and which I understand was where Louis XVI (or XIV) built his palace for himself with miles of wonderful gardens about it. The house of Marie Antoinette was also out there and some of the fellows who managed to get out there said it was well worth seeing.

At night the streets were dark and everything closed except a few theaters. I went one night to the Olympia Theatre which was a combined revue and vaudeville. Heard lots of American music at both. The theatres were certainly palaces of enjoyment and gayety. When you go through the doors you come into a lobby as large as the theatre itself with numerous little tables in the center where you sit and drink with your best girl (if you have one) and a bar. A broad promenade runs around this and an orchestra plays continuously. This is for your amusement during intermissions. In the theatre proper there is also a broad promenade running entirely around it behind the seats where you can also promenade with your best girl (I didn't choose any, although all the soldiers received many invitations to promenade from pretty little Mademoiselles and most of them chose). I enjoyed it immensely and fully resolved to bring you over sometime if possible. That is after the war.

Still through it all I was impatient to get to work and was delighted when orders came one evening to leave for Italy that night. There was no sleeper on the train. I dont think they use them over here, and I traveled in a 1st class compartment which was really fairly comfortable in a pinch. For two nights and two days I rode continuously without changing trains and on the third night got off at the city of Turin, Italy and had a nice shower and bed until 4:30 a.m. when I started again traveling for another night and day until I found myself here. All the way down the train had a most pleasing way of stopping three times a day for 40 minutes or an hour at towns where there were the nicest little restaurants with the nicest meals imaginable, wine and all, already waiting on the table paid for and all.

Coming through the Alps I saw the grandest scenery you can imagine. Great piles of solid rock towering up among the clouds with pretty little green valleys in between. At last I went through a tunnel which took over twenty minutes and is said to be second to the longest in the world and found myself in "Sunny Italy". I think that it is simply great too. So like our own climate only warmer. I was charmed with France but the sun didn't shine over 15 minutes during my stay there so I believe I'll like Italy much better.

Now I am hard at work – not "hard" at work either because it's so intensely interesting no amount of it could be hard, and they won't let me do as much as I want and besides that I'm living off the fat of the land and treated like a conquering prince. Oh but it's great! If I just had you with me now little girl I'd be perfectly happy. But I cant help but miss you tremendously. However it wont be so terribly long before I'll have you with me again. But sweetheart my work here will occupy 5 and perhaps 6 months. Dont worry about that though dearest. Try your best to be cheerful and happy while I'm away. Remember that I'm safe, well and contented and working for you and "ours" and time will pass. Remember darling that you can help me most by taking care of yourself since you are my all. I got your letter saying you were going to see Mother Rollins and hope you didn't forget to buy your clothes as you said. Whenever you feel like it dear just go stay with her as much as you want and if you want to go see Dotte do that too. Hear? Now be real good and don't forget one minute to take care of yourself. I have to stop now. Give some of my love to Mother Dad and Billie and tell them the news. Has Sis come home yet? With a million long long soul kisses and hard tight hugs and all my love

Your Devoted Paul

I'll write often now.

§ THE PRINCE ARRIVES IN ITALY ॰

American pilots joined France's Lafayette Escadrille and another contingent in 1917–18 – the Italian Squadriglia – led by then-Captain Fiorello H. La Guardia.

Italy
Oct. 17th 1917

Dearest Babykins –

I know you are going to be surprised when you find out I am in Italy and you should be tickled to death over it. I am simply <u>delighted</u>. <u>Everything</u> is splendid and I'm treated like a prince. Also now since I'm settled here our plans will very probably work out as we intended but not so quickly as I thought. Italy is a wonderful country. Climate about the same as you are having only warmer. I think I'm the luckiest fellow ever was to be sent down here. Start flying right away.

OCTOBER 17, 1917

How are my babies now? I got your last letter written to Ft. Wood and your first letter since I left. Will get the rest in time. Did you get my cable? <u>Send</u> my sweater and things to the address below dearest and be a good little wife. I'll write you a long letter to follow this note. Love to all – with millions of long, long kisses and hugs and all my love.

Your Devoted,
Paul

[Be sure and get this address exactly correct as it is dear]
  Aviation Instruction Detachment, Itally (*sic*)
  American Expeditionary Force
  Paris, France

  Use only a two cent stamp on letters

§ THE "JOY STICK" §

The American pilots – eager, enthusiastic – were said to be respected and admired by other pilots for their "devil-may-care" spirit.

Italy Oct. 19th

Dearest Babykins –

Well I know it will be good news to you that I'm flying every day now. I've been up four times in the last two days and this afternoon had a splendid 15 minute ride when the pilot let me have entire control of the machine for about a mile. The very first time I went up I found it great stuff. When you go up or fly along a level it doesn't feel any different from speeding along an absolutely smooth auto road so far as I can tell. It is only when you start coming down that you have a

OCTOBER 19, 1917

sort of "lost in space" sensation for a second, and also when you take a steep turn and tip the machine up sideways ("banking" it is called) you get the same "lost" feeling for a

moment. The first time I went up it was only for an 8 minute "joy ride" and it seemed perfectly natural to be flying up there 500 ft. (he only took me up 500 the first trip) above the ground. The machine felt so solid and steady that the ground seemed of no consequence to me whatever. I was going along enjoying it hugely when I suddenly felt the seat drop out from under me turning sideways at the same time. It was some feeling for a second until I felt the seat under me again and got my bearings when I realized that I was going down around a curve and turning sideways all at once and saw we were making a beautiful banked turn and felt alright again. When we got back over the drome I saw my pilot give his "joy-stick" a little push forward ever so little, and again I felt the seat drop from under me. It was only a second before I settled into the seat again and let go my desperate grip of the life belt. Then I calmly noticed the ground rushing up to meet us at a tremendous rate but it didn't alarm me for I could simply "feel" that we were going to flatten out and slow up before we got to it. Sure enough when it was right on us I saw the pilot ease back a mere fraction on the "stick" and we flattened out and settled down without a single bump, skimming along a hundred feet or more and stopping. It was certainly an exillerating (*sic*) feeling. Today as I told you he let me have entire control of the machine part of the time, sitting with his hands on my shoulders and showing me what to do by pushing forward or back or sideways (on my shoulders, I doing the same thing to the "joy stick". It seemed perfectly easy. A few more days and he will let me ride in the back seat and control the engine and rise and land by myself. I'm so tickled with it all that if I had you with me now I'd be absolutely happy. But it wont be so terribly long now dearest before I will have you again. I'd like awfully to have another letter from you to know how my little wife is getting along now. But I just have to wait for it. Be a real good little wife now and write me every time you can and address your letters carefully to the last address I sent you. Take care of yourself now doll. Give some of my love to Mother, Billie and Dad. With millions of long long soul kisses and hard tight hugs and all my love

Your Devoted,
Paul

———

---

§ A NEAR MISS – A WAR DANCE §

The flying temperament was sometimes headstrong
and reckless – easily irritated by encroaching rules
and discipline.

Italy – Oct 22nd 1917

Dearest Babykins –

Got a letter from you yesterday which was written on the
21st of Sept. That is some mail service I'll say but I think they
will come faster after you get my Italy address. Your sweet
little letter with the one enclosed from Mother made me feel
lots better about you. I can't help worrying about you dear
and your letters always make me feel better for a while.

So you changed your mind about going to see Mother
Rollins at the last minute? Well I am afraid you are developing
into too much of a "stay at home". Just like
you tho' sweetness, just a spoilt "pretty baby"
when I'm not around. If Sis comes home tho'
she'll have the whole place buzzing the minute
she "makes a landing". Dearest what are you so busy and in
such a hurry to get your sewing done so early? I didn't think
there was all that rush. You alarm me! You know I wont even
possibly be there Xmas. Just about Xmas I'll be doing my high
flying if we have reasonably good weather between now and
then. I'm flying every day now sweetheart and it is absolutely

OCTOBER 22,
1917

---

fascinating. It thrills a fellow through and through to get out on the field just as the east is beginning to get gray and sail up over the ground. My instructor speaks no English and is very temperamental. He expresses himself by shrugs and jestures (*sic*) better than any man I ever saw before. Yesterday he was coming down landing pretty fast and just as he got about five feet off the ground a pilot in another machine who didn't see him coming "taxied" across right in front of his landing place. My instructor just cleared the machine on the ground by an inch and landed farther off. As soon as he stopped he tore off his gloves, helmet and coat and threw them violently to the ground jumping out and doing a war dance on them. I think I heard some artistic Italian "cussing" too. He refused to go up again and so I thought I wasn't going to get my mornings' flight. By afternoon he was back in a good humor and took me for a very nice lesson. Let me sit on the back seat and do most of the controlling. This morning he didn't want to fly because our regular machine was on the bum having some repairs done. He wouldn't go up until we got our regular machine and then it was too late for me to get a lesson. I think I'll get one this afternoon tho'. In spite of his "temperament" I like him hugely because he is an awful nice fellow. They all say he is one of the safest men in the game. I know he is an expert.

When I first got here I was as you say extremely "over anxious" but got over that in the first two days. After you have spent three hours on the field waiting for a ten minute lesson you get over that being "over anxious". I think I've had enough flying now sweetheart to feel sure that I can make a success of it. It certainly is great. I have splendid accommodations, nice room, real sure enough bed, shower bath and nice table service but am not especially fond of Italian food. However I manage to get plenty to eat. My cigars are a great consolation to me. I've limited myself to one a day to make them last longer. I have worlds of time in which I have nothing to do but "set and talk and smoke and think and sometimes to break the monotony, I just sets".

So on "registration day for women" you are going to register, eh? You haven't a son in the war but a husband, eh? Have you been married long? You talk awful big about it. What ticket are you going to vote? I do think it's a good thing tho' and hope you register.

I guess you are feeling all right again now sweetheart since you didn't mention it. I certainly hope so. You dear, when I said I wanted you to get fat I meant it. You can't get too fat for me now before I get home again. Even if I did laugh at you in N.O. for being so fat I think you were prettier then than I ever saw you before altho' I've never seen you anything but pretty. Honest. You can't tell me you are eating too much, or taking too much care of yourself sweetheart. Be a real good little wife now and dont forget how terrible hard your husband loves you and how important you are to him. Give some love to Mother Dad and Bill. I'll write to Mother later. With a million long, long soul kisses and hard tight close hugs and all my love.

Your Devoted,
Paul

If you haven't already sent my sweaters then do it right away, precious, for they will just about get here in time to be of great use to me when I start going to high altitudes for my tests. Wrap them very secure and address them carefully to the last address I sent. Be sure and enclose some kisses.

❦ WASTED WORRY ❦

Mail from the States was very slow, often arriving six weeks or more late. *War news:* An October 25 battle at Caporetto, Italy, had ended in disaster for the Italian military.

Italy, Oct. 27

Dearest Babykins –

Haven't done much work since I wrote you last as the weather has been too bad for flying. Have had a couple of good lessons however in the last three or four days. There's absolutely nothing for me to do between flights except sit around and smoke and think. I got that pack of pictures we started in Austin, developed and will send you some in my next letter. The photographer asked if you were my sister. Said we looked like each other. I felt very flattered but started to wallop him for insulting your looks. The man here doesn't do very good work.

OCTOBER 27, 1917

I have only received one letter from you, dearest, since I got down here. That was written on the 21st of Sept. We are expecting another batch of mail now everyday and I'm hoping to have several in it for I know you've written more than that one since I left. It comes to us in batches every ten days or two weeks.

I'm perfectly contented and well and very much engrossed in flying. Our instruction comes awful slow tho. Much slower than in the States. But I'm much safer than in the States. Accidents here are just almost impossible. So don't spend a moment worrying your little head over my safty (*sic*) for it would be worry entirely wasted. If you want to worry about anything then worry about your own sweet self for then there would be two worrying about you. Are you going to be absolutely alright dearest until I get back? If you have any doubts then please tell me.

This is just a note today to let you know I am O.K. and doing well. Write me real often and use the last address I sent as I'll be here for four or five months. Be a real good little wife now and dont forget how I love you. Take care of yourself. Give some love to Mother, Billie and Dad.

With a million long long long kisses and hard tight close hugs and all my love

Your Devoted Paul

Address.
Aviation Instruction Detachment Italy.
American Expeditionary Force
Paris, France

𐅟 A CENSOR'S CUTS პ

Talk of Russian or German movements is kept out
of letters home.

November 1st 1917
Italy

My darling babykins —

No more news from you and it is awful hard on me for
I cant help worrying myself to death over you. I've given up
ever getting another word from you dear until the war is over.
I'm trying to reconcile myself to the idea that Mother will look
after you and take care of you until I get out of this pickle. If
I knew that you were getting my letters it would help some
but I feel sure you are not getting my letters nor the cable I
sent now over a month ago and I know the effect it will have
on you. I read in the Paris papers that the army post office in
Paris is enlarging its force in order to assure
the prompt delivery of Xmas mail to American
soldiers. That post office in Paris is an utter
mockery. They never deliver any mail to
American soldiers. They only chuck it into a
corner to collect dust or bundle it up and send it always in the
opposite direction from the owner. If I'm lucky enough to get
back to Paris either during or after the war I'll be able to dig
into the dusty corners of that office and find all the mail you've

NOVEMBER 1,
1917

sent me and if it's not there then it will probably be in some Chinese post office. We get a big bag of mail down here from Paris every few days but never yet has it contained a letter for any man here. It all belongs to some poor unlucky chaps way back in France. Well so much for having given up my mail. I wont know whether you're still alive or not until the war is over dear and I wont even know when you become a sweet little mother. If this letter should accidentally reach you don't let my blues bother you dear for remember I'll be able to stick it out and pull through every thing over here in time and come home "whole and healthy". While I'm in such a cheerful mood I might add that I haven't had a flying lesson for a week and dont expect to have one for another week. If I do get one in the next 10 days it will be simply because my instructor could not invent another excuse to keep from working. Also the food we get here is wonderful. A cup of coffee and slice of bread at 5:30 a.m. Macaroni for dinner and macaroni again for supper with clock like regularity except that one day the bread gives out and we only get the coffee for breakfast and the next day the sugar runs out and we get bitter black coffee and then the coffee runs out and we only get the slice of bread. But the supply of Macaroni is inexhaustible. I hope to pass my air test and get my "golden eagle" by the end of March 1918 when I will according to enlistment be in line for commission but the rumors here now are that the commissions will never arrive. That remains to be seen however. There is also the ever present rumor of a "pay day soon" but never the pay. However I still have money of my own left. Even with all the above conditions are apt to be worse. The Russians are practically out of the war it seems and the Germans have withdrawn large *[There appears to be a censor's cut here.]

And now "can you beat it?" if I could just get some word from you saying you were alright I'd be perfectly contented and full of "pep". So you see you are the whole keynote to my cheerfulness. Just let me get cheerful news from my little wife and it makes me feel like I can whip the German army single handed. In another month I shall do my best to get permission to cable you a cable address for myself so that you can cable me every couple of weeks if you are alright or if anything goes wrong. Then this army mail outfit can go hang itself. Meantime I'll just have to worry myself to death over your welfare and trust to luck you'll be alright dear.

Dont worry about me for I'm alright. Be a good little wife and <u>take</u> <u>care</u> of <u>yourself</u> <u>for</u> <u>me</u> <u>dearest</u>. Give a little love to Mother Dad and Billie. With millions of long soul kisses and hugs and all my love.

Your Devoted Paul

<u>I'm</u> <u>lonesome</u> <u>for</u> <u>you</u>.

I'd ask you to send me some cigars and a humidor of Prince Albert tobacco but I would never get it so don't send it.

❦ BATTLE CRUISERS OF THE AIR ❧

An Italian Caproni was a three-engined bomber aircraft with a ninety-eight-foot wing span and fuselage length of forty-nine feet.

Italy
November 1st 1917

My darling babykins –,

In a "blue funk" the other day I wrote you an awful punk letter due to the fact that I hadn't gotten any mail from you and it was rumored that we were not to have any more mail down here. But yesterday more excitement broke loose here in camp than I've seen since I've been here. It was caused by the arrival of <u>seven</u> sacks of mail. The post office in Paris has at last discovered in some unknown way that I'm down here, for there were four letters from you dated, Sept 24th, Sept 26th Oct 1st and Oct 8th and one from mother dated Sept 30th and one from your mother dated Sept 23rd. My! but how they did dispel the gloom! They revived my taste for macaroni and I'm actually enjoying it now. Everybody got <u>some</u> mail and spirits went right up to a 100 per again.

NOVEMBER 1, 1917

You sweet thing! I didn't know you were making me so many things! You bet I need them. And I really believe I'll get them now if you've already sent them, for since the secret that I'm in Italy leaked out in the Paris post office I wouldn't be a bit surprised if they didn't send all the rest of my mail down here to me. The warm clothes you mention sweetheart sound good to me for it's getting to where it is cold in the air and standing out on the flying field waiting for my turn up in the early hours before sunrise. I hope you fixed them up securely and in not too bulky packages for it is a hard trip for an ordinary package to stand.

You know I added to my last letter that I would like to have a box of cigars and a humidor of Prince Albert but didn't think I would get them. Now I think there is a pretty good chance of them reaching me so I'm going to ask you to send them on. If you can dearest get me a box of El-Roi-Tan cigars, but if they don't have them then send me a box of good mild ones, not too expensive for I might not get them. Also dear get me a carton of Picayune cigarettes or about 50 packages of them and a <u>tin</u> humidor (use to cost a dollar) of Prince Albert pipe tobacco. Make it into a very secure package, well wrapt (*sic*) and if you get it right off I should get it Christmas week. Then I will have plenty of good smokes to last the rest of my time over here for I think they should last. I should finish up here by February dear but may not move from here until March, where, I don't know and wouldn't be allowed to tell if I did. It's too bad sweetheart but there is no help for it. How are my two babies going to be, without me so long??

I've done no flying now for over a week on account of bad weather principly (*sic*) but I'm hoping the weather will get good for flying again tomorrow. Soon anyway. The last flight I had I was progressing fine and it was the best I've had so far. Handled the motor and made a short flight and landing without my instructor touching his controls. Then my instructor took me up about 500 ft. and headed the machine into an awful strong wind that was blowing and let me hold the machine into it for a few minutes. The machine pitched and tipped something awful ("bumping" they call it) but he just left it to me. When he took the controls and landed me I was ready to admit I couldn't land in a strong wind yet. However that will come with practice. I suppose that you have already guessed by my being in Italy that I'm to fly a big Caproni machine. The big battle cruisers of the air. I suppose you've seen their pictures and descriptions in the papers as some New York papers we got in this mail were full of pictures and descriptions of them. I'm well pleased with the idea and have a feeling that the war wont last much longer when I fly one of them over the German lines.

I was imminencely (*sic*) amused at you wondering if I had any fire over here. Why I haven't seen a fire since I left New York. They simply dont have them and in Paris they only allow the hotels to heat water for bathing on Saturdays. Down here they don't heat it at all and you can imagine me taking a freezing shower several times a day! No! Only on warm sunny days which we have here occasionally like our Louisiana climate. But that is a small matter.

Of all the news that lifted the "gloom" dear it was that of my big and little babies. I wont have a blue funk again now unless I go another two months without any news from you. You can't imagine sweetheart how much your cheery sweet letters mean to me. And when you say my two babies are well and getting fat – "Voila"– it makes me happy. I want you to tell me all about your sweet self in every letter, how you feel, what you do and what you think and how much you love me. So you finally got to Mother's, eh. I'm awful glad you did cause I know it will cheer you up. I think I'm missing a terrible lot not to be able to be with you now and see those clothes and guess I will before they are too "old". I like the way you say "thanks sweet Daddy" so much that even if I wasn't there to buy those clothes I think I shall buy you some more when I get back to see if you'll say it some more. I'll write you again soon dear, I have so much to tell you now since I have your letters, this is just to tell you that I'm well, contented and alright and safe. Progressing slowly but surely. Take care of yourself as you would have me take care of myself. You mean more to me than I to you dont you sweet baby, with millions of long soul kisses and hugs and all my love. I wrote to B. & M. and will write to our Mother's Rollins and Potts too. Give some love to Mother, Dad and Bill and tell Bill to write me.

Your Devoted, Paul

The Caproni aircraft

§ GETTING CONTROL &

An aviator needs confidence in order to relax and gain control of his machine. *War news:* At this time in Europe, the Bolsheviks seized power in Russia, thus launching the October Revolution.

Italy
Nov. 7th 1917

Dearest Babykins –

I think I have fairly good news this time for the bad spell of weather has broken and we've had three good flying days in succession with still good weather. I had three fine flights since my last letter, making my tenth lesson and in two more weeks (with good weather) I'll be "soloing", that is flying alone. Also I will pass my second Brevet (final test) before Xmas and get my commission at least by the end of January. Just think, when you get this letter I'll be going up in a machine all by my lonesome "on my own hook". Then is when I'll get up into the clouds. The instructor hasn't time to go up very high with a pupil so consequently a fellow doesn't get as high as he likes until he gets in a machine by himself. And by Chistmas (*sic*) I think I will have passed my last test. In my last two lessons I've had the feeling of confidence that you need before you can

NOVEMBER 7, 1917

"solo", that is you feel entirely in control of the machine and haven't the least bit of nervousness in what you do. I landed alone 8 times in 9 minutes and didn't "bump" but once (on the first landing) this morning. And my instructor seemed satisfied with my performance.

This morning I was very amused at my instructor. Just as we were rising from one landing another instructor with his pupil came into our field of vision headed right across our path. Bassi and I both jerked the controls back and we shot almost straight up, nearly "stalling". The other fellow saw us about the same instant and went down, clearing the landing gear of our machine by about three feet. It happened so quick that I didn't have time to get scared or nervous and Bassi hung over the side and shook both fists at the other machine and "cussed" them at the top of his voice, which they couldn't hear. But one of them shook his fist back at Bassi and it made him so much "madder" that I thought he was about to jump out. He beat himself over the head and fairly frothed at the mouth. When anyone almost runs into him Bassi takes it as a personal insult. He is an awful good instructor, the safest one of the bunch here, they say.

I guess it will be another week before I get any more letters from you but I'm still digesting that last bunch of sweet letters. That picture you sent me is so cute it tickles me. You look like that bunch of babies belonged to you. If you can take any more pictures do send them to me. I'll send some of our pictures in this letter and some in the next, so if you dont get these you'll maybe get the next. Poor little girl, you have an awful hard time sometimes by yourself without me to look after you. You let Mother and Dad both "buldose" (*sic*) you. I <u>bet</u> <u>you</u> <u>do</u>. With Dad, you just have to open up and "buldose" (*sic*) or run right over him, then he gets in a jolly good humor. But never mind sweetheart you tell me all you don't like and I'll see that it's changed. I don't want you imposed on about doing things and going places you don't want to and wont have it. That is one thing that worries me about Bill when I'm away. He gets into so much trouble that I can shield him from when I'm there. It does him lots of good to plan things with me, like a trip to Cou – and I like to encourage him. I hate awful bad to see him with the associates he gets at school, in fact it goes entirely against the grain with me but Mother just wouldn't exercise her authority over him when she had it so now such things cant be controlled. If I get time when I get back I want to take him out on Kisatchie for the "darnedest" week he ever had and you too – provided you can go.

I read our Grandmother's letter and since have been wondering why you are not all vain over who you are. Why I'm all "stuck up" over who you are already. But you are just too sweet, it's not in your nature. Perhaps that is why you've enslaved me. To the happiest slavery there is however. How are my two babies? I'm hoping they're as healthy and "fat" as I am. Don't you worry about me a bit for I'm perfectly safe and alright. Give love to Mother Dad & Billie for me and be a good little wife. With a million long kisses and hugs and all my love.

Your Devoted
Paul.

Am sending 5 pictures of myself, one of them the one we took before I left.

In time of war, keeping in touch with family gives comfort to soldiers.

Italy
Nov. 9th 1917

Dear Mother Rollins –

I have received two letters from you, one while I was in Paris and one since I arrived here. I was awfully glad to get them. A letter is a luxury over here for they come few and far between.

The last letter I received from Shirley, dated Oct. 9th, she was with you and her letter seemed more cheerful and contented than any I've received from her since I've been over here. I know it was her visit to you that did it and I don't see why she doesn't go to see you whenever she feels like it except that she is such a big baby she doesn't want to go alone. It is pretty hard on the little girl being separated from me so suddenly and at such a time but if she can just keep her nerve up and not let anything happen to herself she can rest easy that as sure as the war is bound to end I'll come out of it whole and healthy. I believe that I worry more about her safety and health than she does about me for I'm so afraid something will go wrong with her while I'm away. I just have to do my best

NOVEMBER 9, 1917

to brace up my faith in every thing coming out alright.

I'll leave it to her to tell you of my doings over here (to save work on the Censor) except that I'm flying regularly now and find it the most fascinating work I ever tried. I hope to pass my air tests by Christmas. I like Italy fine, that is the part of Italy I came through on my way down here but I don't like this particular part. The lower class of people around here live too dirty and there are billions of flies but I'm proof against them on account of my inoculations. I'm very anxious to get leave to visit Rome and possible Naples and think I will during or after Christmas. There are so many interpreters here that I don't find it necessary to learn any Italian but I'm doing my best with French.

I'm well and doing fine, making good progress in my work. Write me news of yourself whenever you can & keep me posted on how Shirley is. I'm afraid she'll pretend to be alright when she is not to keep me from worrying.

Yours, Paul

Learning to turn into and out of the wind takes practice; also judging your speed when landing. *War news:* The 100-days-long Battle of Passchendaele (in neutral Belgium) ended in stalemate on November 10.

Italy, Nov. 13th

Dearest Babykins –

I got a letter from both our Mothers yesterday (dated Oct. 11th) but none from you. They both said not to worry about you that you were getting "fat" and as "saucy" as ever. I hope so for that is the way I want to find you when I come home.

I haven't been up any for the last four days as the weather has been too windy and rainy to take out the machines. But I had an awful good lesson the last time I got up. I'm "getting on" to the knack of landing now altho' it is still hard for me to judge the precise moment when I should flatten the machine to the ground. When you are up high you know it doesn't seem that you are hardly more than creeping along and then when you get down near the ground you suddenly realize the speed at which you are traveling. I think I'm getting on to it pretty well however. The turns into and out of the wind still make me pretty shaky also but I've got to the point where I

NOVEMBER 13,
1917

can handle the machine alright in the air. I'll have to have ten more lessons (two or three weeks) before I can "solo". I haven't smashed up any thing yet altho' a number of other fellows have. Perhaps the little medal you gave me to wear for luck keeps me straight. I wear inside my shirt pocket.

The last letter I got from you sweetheart you were at your mother's but I guess you are back home now. Did you enjoy your self out on Boeuf (?) River? Better go all you want now dear for I guess you wont be able to get off much after Xmas. I think of you all the time and wonder lots if you get very lonesome at home without me. But wait till I get back and we will have a good time there.

Yesterday was a holiday (the King's birthday I was told) and myself and another fellow took a long (5 mile) walk across the fields and vineyards (*sic*). We inspected some very picturesque old country residences and got to talking to a sheep herder who "sicked" three of the largest most vicious looking sheep dogs I've ever seen on us. We did some artistic rock throwing too and got away without a scratch. We didn't stop to ask the old fellow what made him "sick" his dogs on us.

I've been thinking of what you said about the place. After the war is all over and I get back to citizen life why nothing would suit me better either, my dear, with you. This flying game is not one that a fellow can take up and stay with it to a "ripe old age". The longer you stay with it the more wreckless you get and past your prime you are not safe!

The way you speak of my mustache you must think it is a veritable "Rip-van-Winkle's" beard. It isn't! It is a very nice neat little mustache. Hardly large or heavy enough to show well in a picture. I'm very vain over it and when I have nothing to do I very often sit and caress it. Just wait until you see it!! I'll leave it to you to say then whether I keep it or not!

Dearest don't worry a bit about me. I live <u>very</u> comfortable. True I'm awful tired of macaroni as a steady diet but it fills one up and keeps you from being hungry. I'll be glad to get the sweaters and things you are sending me for they will make me lots more comfortable and help out in my flying later when I go to soloing.

I will be paid soon and when I do rather than bank it over here or keep it with me I'm going to cable it to you as I don't need it. So cable me a reply when you get it. Use the same cable address as my letters and it will reach me immediately. Also give <u>Will</u> $25.00 of it. You can cable me any time you want and in <u>case</u> <u>any</u> <u>thing</u> <u>important</u> <u>happens</u> be sure to do so, using American Aviation Detachment, Italy, as the cable address. "C?" <u>Now</u> be <u>good</u> and love me lots and remember how tremendously much I love you. Give love to Mother Dad and Will and take care of yourself. With millions of long kisses and hugs and all my love

Your Devoted
Paul

Paul Potts in Italy sporting his new mustache

Fire would be a luxury, as would heated water
for bathing.

Italy
Nov. 19th 1917

Dearest Babykins: –

Just received your letter dated Oct. 20th and your package
of socks, also a letter from Lillian. The socks are <u>very</u> welcome
dear for they are most comfortable and warm to put on in
freezing weather with no fire. You say you don't see how I can
wear them but I sure can, inside of boots, several pair at once.
The home knitted ones, about half an inch thick are the best. I
got one pair like that from the Red Cross.

NOVEMBER 19, 1917   I'm having another long spell of inactivity
dear. Have not flown for a week now and no
telling when I will fly again. The winter has
set in here and just wont permit any flying. All
I can do tho' is be patient and just wait.

Mail is so slow that I wouldn't be surprised if it was over
a month since I cabled you before you got my first letter and I
mailed it at the same time. All your letters to me are a month
old before I get them. And remember in sending me anything
that it will be a month or more before I get it. For that reason
it would hardly do to send me a box or anything for Xmas for it

wouldn't do me any good.

I knew Mother would take you under her wing and take the best care of you she can. But you talk like an invalid just recovering from something. You haven't been sick have you?? I thought you were as well and strong as ever in Austin, only not as fat as possible. I hope you are taking the best care possible of yourself. I guess you've got your glasses by now. I don't mind you wearing them occassionaly (*sic*) but I don't like to think of you wearing them constantly.

Don't worry about me a bit dear for I'm alright, and well and fairly comfortable. The only thing is that during all this winter weather I have nothing to do except sit around day after day and twiddle my thumbs and smoke.

You and Mother take care of yourselves. Love to all. With millions of kisses and hugs and all my love

Your Devoted
Paul

Boys will be boys!

Nov. 23rd 1917
Italy

Dearest Babykins –

Just received your letter yesterday saying that you had received both my letters written while I was in England. I feel very much relieved to know that you at last have started getting my letters, for I knew just how you would be feeling until you did start getting them.

The bad spell of weather we've had here for the last ten days has broken and I'm flying once again. I had a fine flight yesterday and a still better one today. Yesterday Bassi (my instructor) and I saw a rabbit starting across a field while we were up and dived down close to the ground and chased him all over the field. The rabbit couldn't stay in front of us so we chased him going and coming, having lots of fun. Today I got away with some absolutely perfect landings which makes me feel very much encouraged and confident and also which pleased my instructor very much. It wont be very long now, with decent weather before I'll be soloing.

Your sweet letters are very cheering to me and I hope you'll keep them coming just as often as you can dearest. Did you get

NOVEMBER 23, 1917

all the clothes you needed? If you didn't then do so now. Hear? You don't have to tell me they are cute dear for I know that without being told. I always loved your taste in dresses etc. And who can say that I may not be home in time to see you in those very clothes before they're out of date? Now I hope you'll chase around and see Auntie Hollingsworth and any body you want to and not worry yourself a bit about me for by worrying you only hurt yourself and thereby hurt me and dont help me a bit. I'll be just as safe without my worry on your part dear.

But take care of yourself, hear? I'm well and perfectly alright. Give love to Mother Dad and Billie. With millions of long long kisses and and (*sic*) hugs and all my love

Your Devoted
Paul

I'll write again in a day or two when I have more time. Be good.

Congress was slow to pass on giving commissions to officers, at least in the United States Air Service.

Italy.
Nov. 28th 1917

Dearest Babykins –

Haven't had a letter from you for a week or so it seems and of course I'm lonesome for one. Guess the mail is tied up again.

We've been flying every day for a week or more now and I'm thinking that I'll be "soloing" soon for I'm progressing nicely. I've had 15 short lessons now. Time passes awful slowly with nothing much to do. I know it passes just as slow for you tho', although later it will begin to go faster for you, don't you think?

NOVEMBER 28, 1917

I think the matter of commissions has at last been cleared up dear. You know for a while it looked like Congress wasn't going to give commissions after all but now it has been settled that the commissions will be forthcoming after we finish our tests. Some who have finished their tests have already received theirs. This makes me feel very much more encouraged to go on with my work.

The weather is only moderately cold now and I'm not looking for any more real uncomfortable weather such as I've just been through. I had an awful cold and almost had the "La Grippe" before it was over but now I've gotten over my cold and feel as if I had never thought of having the "La Grippe".

I'm predicting that the war will wear it self out by next fall, but of course I'm no authority on the subject. What do you think of it? At any rate dear I should be home by then if only for a visit. I feel like if I ever get home again I'd like to settle down on the plantation with you and never leave it again. How about it, would you like for me to do that??

I wonder what you will be doing Christmas? I may get off to run down to Rome for a day or two. I would like very much to go there and visit all the old historic places in and about the city. I don't know whether I shall be able to get off from here or not yet. I believe this letter should reach you about Christmas or new year so I'm wishing you a very very happy Christmas and New Year and wishing that I could be with you to help make it so. But I'll be with you next time and we'll have something to have a happy Christmas for, then. Wont we? I sent you and the rest of the folks some Italian Christmas cards. I can't send any present for I understand we're not allowed to do so.

Remember that your husband loves you just as much and then some more than you love him and be a good little girl and have just as happy a Christmas as you can with me away. Wish all the folks a Merry Christmas for me and give them some of my love.

With a million kisses and hugs and all my love
Your Devoted
Paul

❦ THANKSGIVING IN FOGGIA ❦

Foggia is on the southeastern coast of Italy on the
Adriatic Sea, south of Rome.

Italy
Nov. 30th 1917

Dearest Babykins's –

I had such a nice flight this morning that I must tell you
about it. It wasn't that it was high or anything extra except that
my instructor didn't correct me once. It was a very successful
lesson and now I'm confident that I can fly the old machine
alone. I made six landings without a single bump. Now in two
or three more lessons I'll "solo". I ought to be soloing inside of
a week with just ordinary fair weather, and by Christmas I'll be
quite an aviator.

November 30, 1917

I had half a day holiday yesterday
(Thanksgiving) and went in to Foggia for
my Thanksgiving dinner which consisted of
beans, fried potatoes, two cheese omelettes
(*sic*), coffee, cheese and toast with a bottle of excellent Italian
wine. I enjoyed it very much and wondered if you were having
turkey. It is quite a treat to wander around Foggia and look at
the <u>ancient</u> buildings and picturesque places. The sights are so
strange and novel. I have not learned any Italian (except a few
words and phrases relating to flying and eating) but I've gotten

to be such an expert at gestures and signs that I can carry on quite a fluent conversation now with a couple of words and my hands. It would make you laugh to see me at it. Everything is so different from our country that I expect I'll act a little strange when I get home until I get use to home again.

What do you know, a fellow who went to V.M.I. with me way back in 1914 is down here with me. Perhaps we weren't glad to see each other. Name is Coupland. The world is very small after all. You don't think so right at present tho' do you dear? But just wait 'till I come home and perhaps take you for a ride in a machine then you will see.

I'm afraid that you think I neglect you in my thoughts for flying since I write so much of flying but dear there is nothing else for me to tell you about. About all I do is fly, now. It's all that happens to me. I do think of you just as much as ever and I keep my promises so stop worrying over me. There is much more for you to worry over about yourself dear. Are you taking as much care of yourself as you would if I were there? Are you getting "fat"? I'm afraid you wont take care of yourself as you should. But if you don't I'll catch you for I'll be able to tell when I come home.

I'm beginning to look for my knitted things now. Every letter I get from you say you've finished them. I do hope you've <u>sent</u> them. And I didn't know you were going to stay away from home so long. Of course Mother wants you. You are her girl now.

I'm looking for my package and some more letters from you any day now. Be a real good little girl. Give some of my love to Mother, Dad, and Billie.

With millions of kisses and hugs and all my love

Your Devoted Paul

Take care of our new "interests" hear? Did I tell you before that I had taken out $10,000.00 life insurance for you under the new insurance act?

———

High altitudes and open cockpits were unbelievably cold, especially in winter. But flying at higher than 12,000 ft. would enable planes to fly over the Alps instead of having to go around them.

Italy, Dec. 9th 1917

Dearest Babykins,

Yesterday was quite a day for me. I received four packages and one letter from you, dated Nov. 5th. The packages were the two knitted outfits and the fruit cake and cakes and nuts. The tin boxes were the very thing to send it in for altho' they were very much bent they kept the contents in good shape. I sampled the cake and it is delicious. All of the eats I'm saving for Christmas but since I had no more American cigarettes and was almost out of the Prince Albert pipe tobacco I have started right in on the smokes. My! But American tobacco tastes good over here. I also started in on the tooth brush and wash cloth immediately as I needed both. I know <u>you</u> think that two outfits of knitted goods are more than I need but you dont know how awful cold it is in the air here in winter. I put them all on at once and then it is not any too warm. Too (*sic*) see a fellow bundle up here for a high flight or a long one you would think he was starting for the North Pole.

DECEMBER 9, 1917

He begins by putting on all the heavy winter under wear he has, usually three suits, then his regular serge uniform with all the sweaters he has and can borrow. On top of all this he puts on big leather breethes (*sic*) lined with wool hair with a big coat of the same material. He puts on three or four pairs of knitted or wool socks like you sent me, a pair of large boots and still another pair of artic (*sic*) over boots if he can get them. He puts on about three pair of woolen gloves with a big pair of leather mits (*sic*) on over them. On his head he puts a couple of woolen helmets like you sent me, wraps a muffler around his neck and puts on his big leather helmet over all so that only his eyes are exposed and a pair goggles that fit down air tight to his eyes protect (?) them. After he gets all this rig on he almost has to be helped into his machine and after an hour in the air if he is not almost frozen he is lucky. I'm glad you saw the flights at the Fair for now you can see how easily it is done. It's only when something goes wrong or a fellows judgement (*sic*) is faulty that there is any real danger.

It was real nice I think for you to meet all my cousins and uncles and aunts in Shreveport and quite natural for them to make a fuss over you. You're such a baby. I'm just as tickled as can be that L.S.N. beat L.I.I. but in one sense it doesn't speak well for L.S.N.'s patriotism. As you know all the fellows in training for aviation are college graduates, that is all over here are, and there is quite a little college spirit in the bunch over here. And we've come to the point where we look on a college who has a winning football team as a bunch of <u>slackers</u>. For if a man is able bodied enough to play college football he is able bodied enough to shoulder a rifle and pack for "Sam". We call all the winning football teams over here "a bunch of slackers".

From the clipping you sent me about L.S.N. I can tell that the war seems just as remote and far away as it did when I was last there. I judge that the funds they are raising for prisoners of war are for the benefit of German prisoners for I cant see how they can assist our own prisoners in Germany. If they could see our own boys in France now they'd put all they could raise on them for, poor fellows, they are not finding life in the rest and training camps in France as near as good as the training camps in the States. I spent a little time in French camps getting down here and tasted a few of the hardships the fellows in the Infantry have to go through, and I'll say that it takes nerve and endurance to stick through the Infantry. Us fellows in the aviation section don't know what hard living is. We have so many comforts and liberties and luxuries given us that the fellows in the Infantry dont get. We are treated like the Lord's own chosen every where we go. I don't guess that the people at home and in thousands of localities just like it will ever have the effects of the war hit near enough to them for them to realize what war is or for them to ever think of it as a reality or anything but a vague thing in which a lot of people they dont know and dont care about are engaged in. Believe me every one on this side of the water realizes and knows what war is. Perhaps later when the lists of "wounded, killed, and missing" begin to be published in their home papers it will help some.

The news that my two babies are getting fat and in good health is awful good news to me. And now if all the coming letters from my babies contain as good news I'll be content, for it is on my two babies health and welfare that my happiness depends. I hope Mary Haynes came to see you for Thanksgiving. She is one fine old girl and was awful nice to me and Piggy Hargrove in Little Rock and I don't blame Dr. McCook for being interested in her. See – I'm right proud of my cousin-in-law.

Yesterday I got an acknowledgement from Paris of the War insurance I took out for you. I took $10,000.00 out for you. Thought it the wisest thing under the circumstances for who can say what might happen. The premium only costs me about $7.00 a month for it.

Tell Billie that when I come home I'm going to bring him

a "peach" of a gun with a few odds and ends for a camp and that we're going to have a big camp hunt. Tell him he'd better save up some money for it.

I wear the little medal constantly dearest and think always of my two babies and the time when I'll return to them and I dont forget my promises. Be a good little wife and have lots of confidence in my safe return. Give some love to Mother Dad and Billie. With millions of long kisses and hugs and all my love

Your Devoted
Paul

§ MY FIRST SOLO ¿

This is a real test of nerves when, for the first time, a fellow must prepare to make life-or-death decisions. Can Paul do it? He'll soon find out!

Foggia, Italy
Dec. 19th '17

Dearest Babykins –

I have your letter, together with Mother's written on the 13th of November. You say you are alright and contented but something tells me you are not. I cannot help but worry about you. I don't believe you like your new home. Do you? Isn't everybody good to you? Tell me what it is. <u>Hear?</u>

DECEMBER 19, 1917

Yesterday was the most exciting, nerve straining day I've ever spent. I "went solo". When the time came for me to take a machine up alone for the first time for a ten minute ride to about 600 ft. I thought it was not going to bother me at all and I got into the machine feeling "cocky" and self-confident enough but I had no sooner left the ground then it all deserted me. I had to hang on to my nerve and self control harder by far than I have ever had to do before to keep my head clear for if I had let my self get confused for an instant I would have been a goner. The first turn I attempted literally scared me out of my wits.

You know when you go to turn you have to ailron (*sic*) into it. That is throw one wing down and the other up to keep from "skidding" out sideways. Well I was going with the wind and started to turn across it. Every time I'd throw up one wing it would just keep coming on up as if the machine was going to turn over with me. I would frantically ailron (*sic*) it down again and go to "skidding" to beat the band. I finally got turned and then with each succeeding turn it was easier. I finally arrived at the place where I could see the big white bull's eye on the field which I was supposed to aim at in landing. Then came a hard time deciding when I should shut off my motor in order to glide down and touch my wheels on that bull's eye six hundred feet below. It was about the hardest decision I've ever made. At last I made up my mind and pointed the nose at that white circle and cut off my motor. I could feel myself drifting to the right in a strong cross wind. Try as I would I couldn't stop that drift and I became alarmed as to where I was going to land. At just about 300 ft. up I seemed to get out of the cross wind and started going straight. I just had time to get the nose aimed at that circle again before I had to forget it in a fight to level out and touch the ground squarely. As I felt the wheels touch and start rolling over the ground smoothly the biggest feeling of relief I have ever had swept over me. I went dashing over the bull's eye about 90 miles a minute in a swirl of gravel and dust and stopped about 400 ft. farther on. I could just feel myself relaxing from that racking strain. The instructor who had been watching me said "alright" only that I had made an awful fast landing. But that is the kind I've been taught to make. I felt <u>very very</u> tired when I climbed out and sat on the ground until my turn should come again. This first flight alone is always very funny to the experienced pilots. A fellow has to go through it himself before he sees the humor in it when he is watching some other fellow take his first trip alone. I went up again later and didn't feel the same at all. I enjoyed my second flight alone fine for nothing bothered me at all. The feeling of suspense and strain had vanished and I did things in a leisurely fashion. This time I didn't roll so far past the circle and made a better landing. I'm a real aviator now, believe me. That's a complete history of my first solo flight and just as I'll never forget the 14th of July, I'll never forget the sensations and nerve-racking strains and excitement of that first flight. Now it gives me a most exillerateing (*sic*) feeling to go up alone. I'm already wishing very much that I had <u>you</u> to stick up in front of me in the "joy seat" and take you up with me. Perhaps I can when I come home.

I got yours' and Mother Potts boxes but haven't got Lillians or Mother Rollins. I received a letter from Mother Rollins yesterday and am answering today as it is "tropo vento" and we are not flying. Now be real good and take care of yourself. And don't worry or be impatient dear. Try to be just as contented as you can.

I have decided not to go to Rome Christmas during the three days holiday we have. I will wait until I pass my second Brevetto and see if I can go then. I have enough "eats" from you and Mother to make Christmas here quite enjoyable. I'm perfectly well and contented and feel that I'm going to be <u>some</u> aviator. Be sweet and dont forget for one moment how I love you and think of you always.

With all my love and a million long hugs and kisses
Your Devoted
Paul

Give some love to Mother, Dad and Billie.

Flying holds great fascination but no pay – that is,
until December 23rd.

Foggia Italy
Dec. 24th

Dear Mother Rollins –

I have just in the last few days received your last two
letters dated Nov. 5, and Nov. 20, but have been spending
so much time on the flying field oweing (*sic*) to a spell of
lovely weather that I'm just getting to an
answer today. Even at that, although I've just
had dinner I've already been up twice this
morning for two very nice flights.

DECEMBER 24, 1917

I haven't been getting my mail regularly of late. Your
last two letters and one from the girl a week ago and one
from her today is all I've had for the month of December.
Her letter of today in answer to my first two letters from
here was a very blue one but bless her heart if she wasn't blue
a little bit I'd be disappointed. I'm as proud of her as can be
for adapting herself to the ways of the family and endearing
herself to them so quickly. I'm sure I know that it's not every
girl who can drop suddenly into a strange family and make
herself at home like my little girl. Even my cold unemotional

Dad has fallen in love with her.

I haven't sent her any money yet for as she has probably guessed I haven't had any. But I'm sending her a $100 this week. Fifty by cable and fifty through the bank here for I just drew some pay yesterday. I think I'll be able to keep some coming to her every month now. I know you've been keeping her supplied and I certainly appreciate it. Dont know what I'd have done without you. In this letter today she said she was going to spend Christmas with you and maybe two or three months after Christmas. When this letter reaches you I suppose she'll be with you and I'm glad for I know she wants her mother when she hasn't me.

I haven't received the box you spoke of yet but I'm sure it will come later. I have Shirley's and Mother's two boxes so I have plenty of good things to eat to make Christmas cheerful. I could have gone to Rome for three days but decided that I'd rather stay here and not miss two days flying and besides Rome might be rather an expensive place to see on Christmas. I can get off for a few days when I have finished my "Secondo Brevetto" (2nd Brevy or final air test) and am waiting for my commission. It will be a better time to see Rome and a quiet (*sic*) inexpensive trip. I'm very anxious to see the places of interest in Rome while I'm in Italy. It holds more interest for me than any other European city except perhaps Paris, and I had the good luck to spend a week in Paris.

I'm progressing splendidly with my flying. I've now completed half the work necessary for my "Prima Brevetto" or 1st air test. I'm already an aviator. I've entirely mastered all feeling of suspense or timidity when alone in the air and am so confident that I can do anything in the air now with no nervousness. I've developed a perfect craze for wanting to be in the air. I'm never so satisfied as when I'm flying. It holds a very great fascination for me.

Tonight being Christmas eve I'm going to town with a

friend for a little supper. I'll be thinking of you and my little
girl and hoping that you'll be having a happy Xmas.
    Watch over the girl for me,

With love
Paul

Shirley's mother, "Mother Rollins"

§ CHRISTMAS DAY EGGNOG §

When the Germans advance on the Italian Front,
the French and English help out.

Italy
Dec. 26th 1917

My dearest Babykins –

I can see from your letter dated Nov. 16, which I received Christmas eve (*sic*) that you are very blue. I wish you could be happy while I'm away dearest, but you know I would be disappointed if you were'nt (*sic*) blue a little over my long absence. There's only one thought you need remember dear and that is that this old war cant last much longer and as sure as it ends and you take care of yourself I'll be back to you. Then we wont be separated any more.

DECEMBER 26, 1917

I enjoyed my Christmas darling such as it was. I flew on Christmas eve. Went up for two flights doing quarter spirals left and right which puts me almost half way through the flying I have to do to pass my 1st Brevetto or test. Yesterday morn, Christmas day, Ed. Smith a young fellow from Mississippi, came over to my room with a "wee bit o' Scotch" and we got eggs and sugar from the mess hall and made some "egg-nogg". We beat the eggs until both our arms gave out (about an hour and a half) but we certainly had some nice fluffy stiff "egg-nogg".

With my fruit cake and eats and a box his mother had sent him we had quite a "Christmasy"(*sic*) morning. Spent the afternoon at a good picture show and the evening in the new Y.M.C.A. that has just been established here, playing the Victrola.

It has been so windy today that there has been no flying and I went up town this morning to send you some money. Had to argue and explain for two hours with the cashier in mixed Italian and English to make him understand that I wanted to cable $50.00 to the Exchange Bank for you. Even now I don't know whether he knows what to do with the 416 lire ($50) he took from me although he charged me $5.00. I entended (*sic*) to send you a draft for 50 more but didn't have any more time today. I'll get it off within a week of this letter tho! I'll be sending you some every month now dear.

That was not the boy I brought out to the car at Ft. Roots who was killed there. His name was Sam Long from Tupelo Miss. Tho' I suspect Long is at Ft. Roots now.

By all means dearest, trot over to Mother Rollins and stay just as long as you like. I know just how you feel. When you cant have me you want her next. Should I come home and catch you away it wouldn't take long for me to chase you back.

I suppose darling you'll be at home when something happens in case I'm not there myself. And there is a good possibility that I cant be there. I'll have to trust you, dear. And please be brave as you know I want you to be. My thoughts are with you always. Can't say more dear but dont forget what you are to me, and your promise.

I'm taking care of myself and there's nothing for you to worry about over me. I'm as safe as can be and there's not a chance of my not coming back to you, and I dont forget my prayers. I've been thinking that you were going to imagine that the Germans were marching right through Italy during this big newspaper scare. I think they did gain 15 or 20 miles but now all is well on the Italian front. French and English are helping out and the Germans cant gain another step.

I wish we could have had this Christmas together but dearest if all goes well with you we'll have the best of Christmas' next year. I often wish when I'm up in the air now that I had you and Will to stick up in the front seat of my machine. Since I do all my flying alone now the front seat looks so lonesome, when I get up high.

I haven't been getting all your letters I know dear and I'm looking for a great bunch of them soon for I've only received 3 in the month of Dec. and I know you wrote me more than that. <u>Take</u> <u>care</u> of <u>yourself</u> <u>now</u> <u>precious and</u> <u>be</u> <u>good</u> and give some of my love to Mother Dad & Billie. With a million long long close kisses and hugs and all my love

Your Devoted Paul

Four inches of snow. It is the first time Paul reports
any heat in his room – from an oil stove.

Italy Dec. 29 1917

My dearest babykins –
Received your cablegram yesterday and it was worth lots
more than it's (*sic*) weight in gold to me. It is so nice, dear, to
have some word from you that has not been a month in getting
to me. It cheered me up more than anything
has in a long time. I sent you one a few days
before Christmas and hoped to have it reach you
in time to let you know during Christmas that I
was alright up to date. The day after Christmas
I also sent you $50.00 by cable that should have taken less than
a week to reach you and I hope you'll write me saying you have
received it. Sending money during these times is an uncertain
business and I cant know for sure that you have received it until
I hear from you.

DECEMBER 29,
1917

There is about four inches of snow on the ground here
but it isn't excruciateingly (*sic*) cold. I have an oil stove in my
room now so that I can keep warm and comfortable in doors. I
am crazy to go up with the snow on the ground to get a bird's-
eye-view of Italy covered with snow but they wont let me today
because of the danger in landing in it. I have hopes of going up

tomorrow tho' if it doesn't melt.

Your cable made me pretty home-sick, but home-sickness is very sweet at times. I pity the poor fellow over here who has no place to be homesick for and no one he loves enough to have a longing ache for. The fellows who have some one at home to want to get back to are the lucky ones.

Some of my friends here who went to Rome for Christmas have come home with glowing reports. They saw the Colliseum (*sic*), Catacombs, Vatican and St. Peters Cathedral and many more interesting old things, relics of times before Christ and Ceasar (*sic*), etc. I am going to try to go down there the latter part of February for I will have finished my "Secondo Brevetto" here by then and will be waiting for my commission to reach me. Of course dear after I get my commission I'll go to the front for a while but that needn't <u>worry</u> <u>you</u> <u>a</u> <u>bit</u> for I've promised to come home safe haven't I? And I should be disappointed to come home to you with out having seen service on the front. But dearest whatever special things you want me to do and see in Rome to tell you about why tell me right away. Someday perhaps we can come over here together and see Paris and Rome with each other.

Now sweet heart are you all right? Trying to get "fat" still? Be a good little wife and take care of yourself <u>above</u> <u>everything</u> for <u>me</u>. <u>Understand</u> <u>dear?</u> Give some love to all the folks. With a million long long hugs and kisses and all my love

Your Devoted
Paul

❦ CUTTING THE MOTOR ❦

It takes lots of practice to cut your motor in order
to spiral down, but it is lots of fun.

Italy Jan 5th, 1918

My dearest little Babykins –

I've received your letters dated Nov. 9th and 18th. The
first one, which had the two cute little pictures in it was a
very cheerful letter and I know my baby was feeling alright
when she wrote it, but the last one dear just worries me to
death. Why don't you tell me, sweetheart, what it is that has
developed? I'm afraid all is not as well as it
should be with you dearest is it? Try to keep   JANUARY 5,
me as well informed as you can precious so   1918
that I wont worry about you.

The two little pictures of my little girl were just the dearest
and sweetest ever taken. If you don't send me some more soon
I'll be apt to forget what a good looking wife I have. Think I
could for one moment? You said you'd send me some of you
and Billie picking pecans so I'm looking for them.

I don't blame you, dear, for getting mad at the girl you
met at the Fair. You know perfectly well that her prediction
doesn't fit <u>me</u>. Nothing is farther from my head. I really didn't
know your curiosity could be stirred up so much as Will H.
evidently had it. Did you find out whether he saw Aimee or

not? I'll bet he took a notion you could find him a girl just like you. Think so?

The "N" sweater arrived yesterday together with a box from my Mother Rollins. The sweater is just what I needed to complete my warm winter clothing. Now I can lounge around my room in comfort. I told you about my oil stove didn't I? Mother Rollins sent me some awful nice candy and some Prince Albert smoking tobacco which certainly touched my heart. Have you sent me the Prince Albert pipe tobacco and the Picayune cigarettes yet dearest?

I get some good pictures with my Kodak every once in a while but I'm afraid to send any because the censor may destroy them. Whenever I get a good one of myself alone I'll send it tho' sweetness. The other nine fellows who left ground school with me are still here and none of them have had any accidents so far. I haven't even broken a brace wire or a single wheel. I'm pretty good when it comes to landing but then my instructor beat it into my head so thoroughly and he could make such perfect landings himself that I find myself not thinking of my landing at all as I come down.

I'm a real live aviator now dear. I can handle my machine as easily as I use to drive the car. The trouble is it seems to tire and exhaust me so. I go up for a few minutes and when I come down and climb out of the machine I'm so tired I have to sit down. I guess I'll get over that as I fly more. The last time I went up I was sent up to climb up to 600 meters or 2,000 ft. and cut my motor off and spiral down. I had a most lovely ride. Took me 10 minutes to climb to 600 meters and maneuver my machine into the proper place to cut my motor and start my spiral, and I sat back and looked the country over good. The ground looks like a huge map under you, every thing flat, and you can see all around for miles on miles. When I cut my motor and started into the first half turn of my spiral I was sorry to have to go down. I like the swirl and rush of a spiral. Am anxious to go up and do another, it's so much fun. Guess I'll get to do a couple tomorrow if the weather is good. I wish more and more dearest that I had you here to take up with me. I know you'd love it. You and Billie. Never mind perhaps I'll take you up back in the States some time.

I think it's a shame to send your "pup" to the plantation. I wouldn't let Dad do it if I were there. Never mind I wont let anyone impose on you when I come home. Also sweetness I'm glad Bill is taking such good care of you. I knew he would but I have got something I'm going to bring him that will tickle him hugely.

I'm glad you can make such good fruit cake for I certainly love it. Next Xmas we'll have us lots of your fruit cake and then you shall make it entirely by your recipe. As far as I can judge next Christmas is surely going to be a merry one for us if you can just take care of yourself dearest and pull through this war without me then all the rest of the wars will have to run themselves for I wouldn't let a million of them take me away from you again you sweet thing. I love you more, more than you do me. Don't I? I cant tell you much about that these days but just you wait until I come home little girl. Hear?

Please dear tell me as much as you can about yourself now for so far your letters are not censored I don't think. This last letter worries me lots. I know that everything is not just as it should be. I have to trust to our two Mothers to bring you through your ordeal safely for me. And it is certainly hard on me not to be able to be with you dearest. Don't forget what you mean to me dear and be good. Give a little love to Mother Dad and Billie and with a million long long soul kisses and hugs and all my love

Your devoted
Paul

Wrote Mother Rollins today and have written her a dozen times before. She must have them.

73

PASSED FIRST BREVETTO

If, at 3,000 ft. for 50 minutes your hands and feet
feel frozen, what must 15,000 ft. feel like?

Italy, Jan. 12th 1918

Dearest Babykins –
Received five letters from you yesterday, dated Nov. 21,
24, 28 and Dec. 1, and 4th besides one from Mother dated Nov.
20th and several from her enclosed in yours. So you see dear
it was quite a banner day for me. The letters came as a sort of
reward for passing my 1st Brevetto or 1st air test yesterday too
and now today I'm on the Secondo Brevetto
that is doing the flying that is a preliminary to
taking the second air test which makes me a
regular flyer and entitles me to a commission.
Yesterday morn it was real cold, snow on the
ground in patches, and I had to stay up over 3,000 ft. for fifty
minutes doing part of my test. My hands and feet almost froze
but my machine was a good one and I didn't have to worry
and nurse it along as I did the other day with a bad machine
so in spite of the cold I enjoyed myself immensely. Now I've
finished all my low work. I go to pretty high altitudes hereafter
gradually going higher each flight until I reach the limit that
this type of machine will climb to. In a month I'm counting on
getting to 15,000 ft. and I may get even higher.

JANUARY 12,
1918

The pictures of you and Billie on the plantation were just as sweet as could be and make me awful homesick. But sweetheart I cant see where you are getting a bit "fat". You just <u>think</u> you're getting "fat", but you just wait until I get home. If you ar'nt (*sic*) "fat" then you had better watch out.

I think you stay pretty cheerful dear and it makes me feel much better to think of you that way. I know what worrying and being unhappy will do for you and it worries me also dear. Just think of how I love you and how I think of you all the time and what a life we'll have when I come home. Don't worry so much about the time I'll come home for I can't tell when that will be but don't doubt for a moment that I will come home for you see dear I have so much to come home for.

I have a pretty good life over here dearest but don't you let anybody make you think I'd stay over one moment longer than I have to and there's nothing for you to worry about over me. You know I'd told you that I cabled you fifty and was going to send you more. Well dear it is so risky to send money that I'm going to wait until I get to Rome to send you more so that I can send it with some safety. I hope you can make out alright sweetness. I'll write again when I have more time. With a million long long – kisses and hard tight hugs and all my love

Your Devoted Paul

High altitudes can affect pilots, owing to the lack of oxygen which could make them lightheaded. It is also extremely cold.

Jan. 23. 1918
Italy

Dearest little Babykins:-

I haven't written you for at least a week and so today I've decided that war or no war my two babies must have a letter so I'm taking time to write.

Since my last letter dear I have had my hands full. It has been beautiful weather and you know beautiful weather to us means "fly". I believe the Italian spring is about to begin here.

JANUARY 23, 1918

I've been accomplishing a good bit of my second Brevet work and in another week or ten days will do my long cross country flight (about 240 miles), and so complete my last air test which will make me a licensed aviator and an Italian military aviator entitled to wear the Italian gold eagle on my left breast. As soon as I pass my test then my name will be sent into Washington for a commission but how long it will take the commission to reach me I can't say. All my flying is for altitude now. A thousand, three thousand or even six thousand feet seem only childs (child's) play to me now. I go up among the clouds now. Yesterday afternoon I was ten thousand feet up. I'm disappointed about the clouds. When you get close to them you find they are only banks of fog or mist after all and don't look near as pretty as from the ground. Some of my fellow flyers say it is gorgeous among them when you can catch the sunlight on them at the right angle but I've never caught it just right yet. I was relieved when I reached ten thousand to find that the altitude in no way affected me. Except for the cold I was just as easy and comfortable as when on the ground. Some fellows feel faint when when (*sic*) they get that high and the thin air seems to bother them but it doesn't feel any different from flying down low to me.

I often think of my two babies and wish for them in the front seat when I'm up high. It is the most isolated feeling in the world. You are completely detached and cut off from the rest of the world. The delicate frame work of linen and wood with the roaring engine becomes your whole world. Almost always when a fellow comes down, the second he climbs out of his machine he begins prattling away as fast as he can talk scarcely knowing what he is saying. Just the relief from the loneliness. Then when he talks down he hunts a quiet spot to sit down and rest and hasn't a word more to say to anyone. Just shuts up as suddenly as he began talking. It's funny but I do it myself without thinking about it.

I just yesterday received your letter written on Oct. 30th dear. It came down from Paris with some old mail they had neglected there. You know it had the little Catholic badge in it. I have received numerous letters of a later date from you. Thanks for the little badge dear and I shall wear it with the other. I don't know any Catholics among my associates but as soon as I find one I shall ask him about it. Also sweetness I received your nice little package of pyjamas (*sic*), cigars and chocolate. I had bought me a suit over here but still the others will come in nicely. As for the cigars and chocolates, why you sweet thing I owe you a thousand kisses for them. And perhaps in a few months I can pay. "<u>C</u>?" I'm smoking one of the cigars now and it makes you seem very near.

Sweetheart I worry about your health and wellfare (*sic*) all the time. I just can't help it. The mail service is <u>so</u> inadequate I only get your letters every three or four weeks apart. You must tell me all you can about your health whenever you write dear. I'll certainly be glad when this old war is over.

I'm sending you a couple of pictures. One of myself in a little Italian donkey cart with a little fellow from Princeton U. standing by. The other of myself (me) in my fur lined leather flying suit and boots just as I dress for my flights. The big head helmet that I have in my hands straps over my head and protects it from the wreckage in case of a smash. It is made of cork almost an inch and a half thick. The absence of my machine in the picture is because I understand the censor will take out my picture that shows a machine. I hope these two get to you. <u>Please</u> <u>note</u> <u>mustache</u> <u>in</u> <u>both</u>! <u>H'm</u>!

I must stop now sweetheart. Be a good little wife and take care of yourself. Give a little love to Mother Dad and Billie. With a million long long kisses and hugs and all my love.

Your Devoted
Paul

I'm perfectly well and healthy and safe.

Tests are conducted for altitude after an hour and a half, and for climbing in 45 minutes. Next comes the 240-mile cross-country.

Italy
Jan. 31, 1918

My dearest Babykins:-

Your three letters dated Dec. 14th, 15th and 16th arrived yesterday. I was on my way to the hangars to fly and so had to put them in my pocket to read when I came down. So they went up with me to 12,000 ft. and I felt almost like I really had you with me.

JANUARY 31, 1918

I know you were all wrought up over not getting a letter for so long and imagining all kinds of things about me dear but you shouldn't. As long as I'm over here sweetheart the mail will be subject to those long delays and you must be just as patient as you can. Of this dear you can rest assured, if anything happens to me you will be cabled immediately. I've made arrangements for that, so if you should go for months without any letters you can still be sure that I'm safe and sound and that my letters are just being delayed. So hereafter dear when you don't get your letters don't worry your little self to death for you may still know that I'm alright.

I received a letter from Mr. Aswell telling me about the War

Risk Insurance and how to get it, enclosing Mama's letter to him. It was wise of you all to take steps to get it taken out but luckily I got the data down here about Nov. 11th and immediately took out $10,000 to you. The number of my application is <u>3972</u> just in case anything should happen to me and you should need it. Also the address is Treasury Dept. War Risk Insurance Bureau, Washington. I can safely say tho', Babykins, that you wont ever have to use that address. I just took it out as a sort of "Safety First: proceeding. "C"?

I'm glad to know you at last got the pictures. I was afraid the censor might not pass them. I sent you two more in my last letter before this one and you can see my mustache alright in them. I'm afraid you were "kidding" me about seeing it in the first ones. Now weren't you, rascal? The fellow in the picture with me on the boat is not Stone but Norman Sweetser the son of a New England minister. He is a graduate of Columbia U. and a very nice young fellow. He came from Texas with me. Stone has been moved to another school and I only see him every few weeks now. My "bunk mate" is a young lawyer from Macon, Ga. named John Ross and he nearly talks me to death. My chum down here tho' is Douglas Farquhar from Maryland. He and I have been through our training together and are now going to take our cross country flight on the same day. I've enclosed a picture of myself and him together out on the flying field. He is a "devil of a fellow" for looks but is just as fine as they make them. We've been competeing (*sic*) against each other in all our altitude work. We were sent up in different machines at the same time for our hour and a half climb to see how high we could get and both came down afraid the other had got the highest. When we compared barographs we found we had both reached 4,000 meters and couldn't get any higher. Then yesterday we were both sent up to climb for 45 minutes to see how fast we could climb. We came down again and found we had both reached 3200 meters in that time. Now day after tomorrow when we do our cross country of 240 miles or "raid" as it is called we will see which can reach the highest altitude on our trip. After that cross country I'll have nothing to do for awhile until my commission reaches me from Washington so he and I are going down to Rome for three days to see all the relics of the ancient days there and the Vatican and St. Peters Cathedral. I'll write you all about it.

Dear your letters cheer me up immensely for they make me feel that my two babies' health is alright and that I don't need to worry so much about that. I know you have been having a trying time at home dear, and that worries me too but if you can just stand it a while remember that I'll smooth everything out when I come back and take such good care of you that I'll make up for being away so long. No dear I'm really sure that I can't get home in April but what I'm not sure of is just when I will be home. I can't see how this war is going to last through next winter and even at that I think I'll be able to get a leave before then. I'd give all I own, and you know it, to be with you right now. But what must be just must and so I can't. The best I can do is to promise you that I will be back sooner or later. So please dear just settle yourself to be patient and think of the time when I will come.

I'm enclosing the post-card picture you asked for.

I'm afraid they are mistreating you at home. My place there is yours and I'm going to write Mother and tell her so. You are just like Mother about letting people impose on you. I've imposed on your sweet nature myself, but I dont want and wont have Dad or Lillian doing it.

Now be a sweet little wife and try to be contented until I come home, and stand up for your rights when any body imposes on you. Dont forget an instant how I love you and take care of yourself for me.

Tell Billie I was certainly glad to get his letter and am answering right away. Give a little love to Mother Dad and Billie. With a million long long kisses and hugs and all my love

Your Devoted, Paul

CIGARS, CIGARETTES AND PIPE TOBACCO

Feb 6th 1918

Italy

Dearest little Babykins –

I received your letter dated Jan. 5th and one from Mother dated Jan 7th with the pictures in it. Also received a letter from Sis dated Dec. 9th telling me of a box she had sent but I didn't get it. I received the box or package from you dear with the scarf and cigarettes and now I'd like to give you a kiss for every one.

So Dad thought I was getting pretty particular about my taste for cigars did he? Well I dont blame him. I'm going to be very sparing of these so they will last a long time, especially now since I have plenty of cigarettes and also the pipe tobacco which is coming. I wont need any more tobacco now for quite a while. Oweing (*sic*) to heavy clouds for the last few days I haven't completed my cross country flight as promptly as I thought I would but I will do it tomorrow or day after. Otherwise everything is well with me dear so dont worry a bit.

I notice you spoke of my Christmas cable dear which I sent you on the 18th of December but you say nothing about receiving $50.00 which I cabled to you on the 26th of Dec. Now I'm getting worried about that 50.00 for it seems to me you should have received it by Jan 5th. That was the very

FEBRUARY 6, 1918

reason I haven't sent you any more money sweetheart, because of this slack way they handle it over here. Although I have a receipt for it the bank here tells me that if you dont receive the money they will write to the bank there to find out why but they wont pay the money back. In other words I may get my money back in five or six years after the matter has been thrashed out thoroughly. I'm still hoping you get it, but I'm going to make these people trace it to see.

Those pictures are treasures to me. Wouldn't take any thing for them. My goodness! But you are getting as fat as a pig. I believe you're as fat as you were that summer down in New Orleans. It makes me happy to see you that way and I hope you dont fall off before I get home. I'm afraid you will tho for that youngster will be awful trying on you without me there and how I wish I could be with you and him now. See?

You alarm me sweetheart talking about what all you do. I don't like the way mother lets you do so much. I wish Ella hadn't left and I do hope you get somebody in her place. Then you horrify me talking about letting Sis crowd you out of my room and make you move upstairs! The idea! No sir you shain't (*sic*) do it. I (?) writing mama about it. And dear, as for your going some where else for April, please don't, I know mother wont let you. Understand? You make me feel like you are being frightfully imposed on in my absence and I know mother wouldn't do it intentionally.

Dont worry a bit more about cold weather for the cold is all over with down here. I think spring comes a little earlier here than at home for it is getting much milder weather and the natives tell me it wont be cold any more. I'm in the best of health. Of course I'm not in quite as good physical condition as at home, for I'm not entirely used to this food yet and dont take near as much exercise as I did in Austin or at home. But I'll still pass and then some.

Now that Christmas is over with I'm hoping that our mail may be a little more regular. I have much to do today dear so

must say bye bye for the present. Be a sweet little wife and
dont let anything happen to my two babies. Give a little love to
Mother Bill and Dad. With millions of long – kisses and hugs
and all my love

Your Devoted
Paul.

Hope you get the two pictures I sent you in the letter
ahead of this.

❧ PASSED SECOND BREVET ❧

Flying regularly plays on one's nerves. The time a pilot spent in the air was about two to four hours, either climbing (top range 12,000 ft.) or making long, gliding descents.

Feb. 9th 1918
Italy.

Dearest Babykins –

Just a short note to let you know I'm still "O.K." Having passed my Second Brevy, thereby finishing my flying for a matter of six weeks or so while I wait for my commission to come from Washington I'm going to take that little three day trip down to Rome I've been telling you about.

I wrote mother about passing my test yesterday.

Sweetness I received a letter from you yesterday dated Dec. 8th. How is that for prompt service? A few days ago I had already gotten one dated Jan. 5th. This mail service is a joke, dear, so you mustn't ever worry when you dont get my letters for it will simply be due to delays in the service.

FEBRUARY 9,
1918

I'll be thinking of you constantly in Rome and wishing you were with me to enjoy it, but perhaps dear I'll bring you over someday after the war is all over and our "snookums" is big enough. It's truly a relief to rest up from flying for a while after you have become a sure enough pilot. I feel the need of a quiet rest for my nerves now for regular flying certainly keeps them

on edge and wears them out. Course inside of ten days I guess
I'll be crazy to get in a machine again.

In Rome I'm going to take some pictures and visit the
Vatican and St. Peters and all those old historical places and
when I get back I'll write you all about them. Now be a good
little wife and take the best care of my two babies, so I wont
worry so much about them and dont forget for one instant how
I love you and what you are to me. Give a little love to Dad,
Mother and Billie and be good.

With a million long long – kisses and hugs and all
my love.

Your Devoted
Paul.

Feb. 11th 1918

Dearest Babykins-

Just a short note from here this morn in an idle moment. "Dug" and myself have to rush considerably to see even a smattering of every thing. We have already been through the Catacombs, driven long the Appian (*sic*) Way, seen the Colliseum (*sic*), the Palatine, Nero's old palace you know, the Forum, St. Peters the Vatican and the Sistine Chapell (*sic*) in the Vatican not to mention all the old arches and part of the old wall.

FEBRUARY 11, 1918

It is very interesting and I have fully made up my mind dear that I must bring you over here sometime and go through it all together again.

St. Peters and the Vatican are absolutely grand but I'll have to wait until I have more time to tell you of them.

Yesterday afternoon we went out to tea at Ambassador Page's house here and enjoyed the treat of once more seeing and speaking with American ladies in real American. Then later we went to the Opera (Falstaff) and had another treat for the music and voices were splendid.

This morning we are going to buy a few things we need and take some pictures in the Colliseum (*sic*) and Forum. I'd give just worlds to have you over here with me but suppose I'll have to wait until I get back home.

Be good and take the best care of my two babies and give love to Mother Dad and Billie. With millions of kisses and hugs

Devotedly
Paul

§ REPORT ON ROME §

Italy.
Feb. 16th 1918

My dearest Babykins:-

I have had to take a couple of days off since my return from Rome to recuperate and get use to the hardships of camp and war again. I found two letters from you dated Dec 25th and Dec 30th and one from Mother dated Dec 30th. I am surely pleased that you had as nice a Christmas as you did and my dear I can assure you that next Christmas will be all that you desire and I know what that is. Dont I?

Rome was simply wonderful. I wrote you a short note while there but of course didn't have time to tell you much about the place. I know you would be interested in St. Peters and the Vatican. I went through both and St. Peters is surely the most wonderful cathedral in the world. Absolutely grand. I saw the tomb of St. Peter inside too with the little golden casket his bones are said to be in, also the throne or place where the Pope sits when there are services. In the Vatican, which is not impressive from the outside as is St. Peters, I saw the most wonderful statuary and the original old masterpieces of Raphael and Michelangelo on the walls just as they left them. There was also the Sistine Chapel in the Vatican whose walls are simply covered with the original paintings of Michelangelo. My ambition is to bring you over here some day when the war is over and forgotten and go

FEBRUARY 16,
1918

through Paris and Rome together. It should be quite a start for our "Snookums" shouldn't it??

Of the old Roman ruins, I can't say much. They were very, very interesting to me but I cant begin to describe them. I took a bunch of pictures of almost every thing and shall send you some when I have them developed. I gazed on the ruins of old Nero's palace and also Julius Caesar's and stood on the spot in the Forum where Brutus made his famous speech to the senate on the death of Caesar. Then I saw Nero's royal box in the Colliseum (*sic*) or rather the ruins of it, the box of the Vestal Virgins, the dungeons and tunnels under it where the prisoners were kept and the tunnels leading from the menageries where the animals used for killing and devouring the prisoners were. As I say it was remarkably interesting and free from fakes. I think there is a law over here which prevents anything being changed about the old ruins.

Every where we went we were besieged by guides. Poor fellows they are having a hard time of it since the rich American tourists come no more and if you dont watch them they will charge the very clothes off your back. We passed them up until we found one who offered to show us the Colliseum, Forum and the Palantine (*sic*) (Nero's and Caesar's old palace) all for what corresponds in our money to a dollar and a half, and by the way that's as cheap as you get them. He pointed out every thing and gave us quite a bit of the old history of it.

Then the Opera, the first real Opera I have had the opportunity of seeing you know, was simply splendid.

At the hotel it was funny when we went to leave the way we were forced to tip every servant who so much as opened a door for us while there. They simply lined up with their palms out. Farquhar almost had heart failure when after he had given the head porter his tip, what he took to be the same one presented himself for another, but it turned out that the mail clerk was a twin of the head porter, hence the mistake in identity.

Even with all this the hotel and living expenses are only

half as much as in our country. Before the war they must have been remarkably cheap. Everything was very worth while and interesting, but the trip on the train was terrible. Had to go and come on a night train and sit up all night in a stuffy little car like a street car at home. That is the biggest drawback to this part of the world I think. The way they have to travel. Our common chair cars would be called palace cars over here.

As I told you sweetheart, for the present I've finished flying, that is passed my Brevy and am waiting for my commission. In a short while my commission will reach me and I'll start flying one of those big Capronis you've probably seen pictures of in the papers. They remind me of a big battleship and I like the way they fly. If there are any in the States when I come home and I can I'll take the whole bunch up at once. Wont that be great?

It is quite a comfort precious to know my two babies are so well. I dont know how I am going to stand not being able to see my Snookums. It is pretty hard, but the war has an end. I'm trusting you to take the very best care of yourself and our little one until I can come and take care of you both. Be a sweet little wife now, give some love to Mother Dad and Billie. With millions of long – kisses and hugs and all my love

Your Devoted
Paul.

I'm very lonesome for you.

———

❦ WEARING THE GOLDEN EAGLE ❦

Italy, Feb. 21st 1918

My dearest Babykins –

Just received your letters of Dec 21st, 24th, 25th and Jan 23rd and also Mother's letters of Jan 19th and one from our Mother Rollins. Also the pair of socks and soap, which I was glad to get.

Your latest letter dear of Jan 23rd is very, very cheering to me. You talk so encouraging of your health and future well-fare that it comforts me more than I am able to tell you. You know dear I cannot help it but that is the source of my greatest worry.

FEBRUARY 21,
1918

If I could just be sure of your future health I wouldn't be bothered a bit. It is the hardest thing in the world for me to have to trust you in any hands but my own. I'm certainly relieved to know you got that 50.00 I cabled you. I had begun to think that I was just out that 50.00 and was on the point of going down to the bank here and raiseing (*sic*) holy sand with a certain fat slick banker I know. However I shall send you more soon but will tell you when I do.

So you had then just received my letter telling about my first flight alone and here I am now, a finished pilot wearing my gold eagle and waiting for my commission to reach me from Washington. I have made so many flights since that first one that now all the novelty has worn off and going into the air is just like stepping into the car to go down town. However I'm having a good long rest from it while I'm waiting for my commission.

I'm enclosing four pictures, sweetheart, one of Farquhar and I in Rome in the Colliseum (*sic*) and another of ourselves in the Forum and one of myself on the flying field some time ago during a cold spell. I can send it to you now without worrying you since the warm weather is here to stay now and the picture is a thing of the past. It just explains how "sunny" Italy isn't always "sunny". I'm sending a small picture of "Daddy" also, wearing his noted mustache which, by the way, is a mixture of choice brindle and red in color and very glossy. It is intended to make my appearance so ferocious that every time I meet a German in the air he at once takes to his heels and saves me the embarrassment of having to fight him. I can then chase him at my leisure.

Yes sweetheart, I got your cable and Mother's box and my Normal sweater and one box of cigars, my scarf and a carton of cigarettes but no box from Lillian or Prince Albert tobacco. Also one of your letters said Auntie was sending a box but if she did I didn't get it. And as for letters I'm sure I haven't gotten 1/3 of yours my dear, but I guess we have to put up with it. I'm just as well and healthy and safe now as if I were at home and although I'm very lonesome for my two babies, dearest, I'm just as contented here as I could be any where away from you. So sweetheart if you let yourself worry about me it will be worry wasted for there is not a thing for you to worry over as far as I am concerned. You are the one who can be worried over, for I'm never sure that you're perfectly alright. Be a very sweet little wife (as you cant help being) and take good care of my little and my big baby and dont forget for one instant how much you are to your husband. Love to the folks. With a million long-kisses and hugs and all my love

Your Devoted Paul.

Remember me to Mr. Dominique if you see him, dear. Be good.

❦ UNLIMITED CONFIDENCE ❦

March 1st 1918.

Italy.

My dearest Babykins –

I have your letters of Jan 23rd and 30th and it makes me feel very much better to have a letter dated so late as the 30th.

Yes, dear, the clipping was referring to my bunch, in fact I know both fellows mentioned and although it exaggerated a little it was true. However those fellow's experiences have been supplanted many times since by other experiences some of which I'm sorry to say were not as lucky. For instance my friend Smith has a "busted" leg and is the most cheerful "crip" I ever saw. He is allmost (*sic*) alright again now tho'. We are undoubtedly the luckiest bunch in the game. My sheer luck surprises me even.

I got your two boxes dearest, the one with the candy and pecans and the one with the, sweater, socks, garters, tooth brush, paste and soap together. The candy was simply delicious sweetheart. Didn't know you could make such good prauleins (*sic*), and you needn't think the difference in color in the sweater is enough to keep it from being a fine sweater. I think you are a wondeful (*sic*) "darner" as well as a "knitter". But sweet heart you mustn't send me any more knitted goods now for the cold is over and I have the greatest plenty now.

And bless your heart you still think I'm doing my washing when I'm really living a very indolent lazy life. We created such

MARCH 1,
1918

a demand for a laundry that one just "sprung up". And dear the only hard thing I have to do is get up at six o'clock when I have absolutely nothing to do. I'd like to be able to lie in bed until at least eight during this time when I'm not flying, but no, I <u>have</u> to get up at the ungodly hour of <u>six</u> to sit around and wait for the day to pass

Your two letters of Jan 16th and 20th just came in dear and I see my two babies were in good spirits then. I dont know what to think of Bob & Margaret. All I can say is "can you beat it"? Yes I remember Toma Williams and I certainly sympathize with him. Just like V.L. tho'. He is still at his petty snide tricks. What I dont understand is why Toma was not in the service somewhere. He always appeared to be perfectly able bodied and no slacker, to me.

You think I don't spend much time thinking about you and our future dear, but I do spend lots of time thinking about just that. This war is not all excitement and thrills. The excitement only comes in bunches, periodically. And I do realize our future just as much as you sweetheart but you simply have to wait until I come home for me to tell you about all my thoughts for I cant write them. Dont you understand? By the time this letter reaches you dearest I'm hoping that our little aviator will be a reallity (sic) and I will be the proudest fellow in the world and wont have to worry so much about you any more.

I can understand your feelings about me exactly sweetheart. You think I'm taking risks all the time and am never safe, but on the other hand it's seldom that I'm taking any risks. But risk or no risk a fellow has to do his duty, and forget the risks. In the flying game if a fellow thinks much about what can happen and tries to avoid it he's no good. The best way is to have unlimited confidence in your luck. And so far my luck has been wondefully (sic) good to me. I'm absolutely sure it's going to carry me through.

The insurance is perfectly good, dear. I dont know that you need anything like a receipt for it to be good. But as soon

as I get my commission and rank as an officer I will try to find
out about it. You see it is not a civilian insurance company. It is
government insurance and therefore good. You needn't worry
about it a bit.

I think it's a shame dear that I cant be with you now, and I
know I'll worry myself sick until you are alright. It's just about
as hard on me as it is on you dearest for I love you so, and you
are so necessary. I'm just trusting – Be a good little wife and
take care of my two babies, for me. I'm well and alright. Love
to Mother Dad and Billie and with a million long – kisses and
hugs and all my love for my two babies

Your Devoted
Paul.

———

96

Italy.
March 10th 1918

Dearest Babykins –

I've just got a letter from Mother Rollins telling me of her plan to have you go to Culpeppers in Monroe instead of staying home with Mother Potts. Either way you want dear is perfectly alright with me. I hadn't thought before of your going to Monroe you know dear, so I think I suggested before that you stay with Mother Potts. She will be awful disappointed I know to have you go.

I know you haven't enough to pay expenses so guess you'll have to draw on your Mother until you get what I'm sending. I know you've been drawing on her before and now really sweetheart you'll make me angry if you dont use what I send you and quit calling on her until I dont send you enough. Now hear? Pay your own expenses in Monroe down to the last dollar I send you.

MARCH 10, 1918

I'm enclosing a draft for $100.00 on the Shreveport Commercial National from the Credito Italiane here and you can cash at any bank where they know you. If you dont stop using your mother's money you'll make me think you have a little Jew in you so quit it and tell me frankly if I send enough to meet your needs. Hear? Dont worry the tiniest bit of a minute about me dearest for I'm just as fat and healthy as can be and living a life of indolent ease while I'm waiting for my commission. Also I'm studying a little French from an Italian and actually learning a little of it.

I'm missing my little girl lots' and would give the world to be with her, but you know that don't you dear? And I have great faith in our two mothers' and my little girl making everything come out right.

Your mother promised to send me a cable and it will be a life saver to me. Remember what you mean to your boy and take the best of care of yourself. Hear? Be good. With millions of long – kisses and hugs to my two babies and all my love

Your Devoted
Paul.

Write me immediately if the draft enclosed in this letter reached you alright. Love P –

Italy, March 12th 1918.

My dearest Babykins –

On March 10th I sent you a registered letter containing a draft for $100.00 for your use in Monroe in case it reaches you in time and in a few days (as soon as I get last month's pay) I'll send you another for $50.00. Be sure and mention if you receive them in at least two letters. That will be all I can send then for six or eight weeks.

Yesterday eve my long looked for commission arrived and at 5 o'clock I took the oath of office and signed up the papers of exceptance (*sic*), put on my officers togs and insignia and became a full fledged 1st Lieut. A.S.S.Q.R.C. I was certainly relieved to get it for Pershing is raising Cain with the Aviation Section. He has recommended that there be no more commissioned pilots, no promotion of officers and no more flying pay for the Aviation. Now that I have my commission his recommendation that there be no more commissioned pilots doesn't affect me, for I'm already a commissioned pilot, but when

MARCH 12, 1918

he recommends that there be no more promotion it does affect me and the flying payable. It means that I can't be promoted to a Captaincy except under exceptional circumstances, for which I dont give a Continental ----!. I'm satisfied for the present with a 1st Lieutenant. But you know a 1st Lieutenant's pay on foreign service is about $190.00 and his extra pay for flying should make it $245 approximately, so you see he cuts me out of about $55.00 per month when he recommends that flying officers no longer receive extra pay for flying. However dear, we are fixed very nicely as it is, so we dont have to worry about John J's recommendations.

I celebrated my commission by lying (*sic*) in bed this morn until eight o'clock (*sic*) and it was certainly luxurious. If you were just alright now, I'd be perfectly satisfied with the war.

By the way, dear, my pay as a lieutenant doesn't start until I get my active service orders from H'dq's. and it will be three weeks before I get them. My acceptance of my commission has to go back to Headquarters in France and when they get it they send my Active Service orders and my pay starts when I receive them. As I said this takes about three weeks and that's why I cant send you anything more for six or eight weeks.

I'm sending you a cable today, so let me know if you got it. I suppose you will get my letter before this telling you that it will be perfectly alright with me for you to go to Monroe according to Mother Rollins plans. You all know what's best over there darling and I want you to suit your own little self. Hear? So do.

I'm hoping that everything is alright with my babies but I cant help worrying about them As for myself you have absolutely not a thing to bother about me. I'm not flying yet awhile, and in the best health and spirits now.

When I was in Rome I got a book to paste my Kodak pictures in and I'm getting quite a collection for my babies when I come home. I have some left over that I'm sending you in this letter, (9 of them) and I'm afraid most of them are duplicates of some I've already sent you. You can pass them around to the folks.

Now be a good girl and take the very bestest (*sic*) care of my big baby and my little baby and be just as cheerful as you can about my being away from you dear for remember I'm with you in thoughts every instant. With millions of long – kisses and hugs and all my love to my two babies

Your Devoted Paul.

❧ AN AIR RAID WARNING ❧

Check $50.00 Enclosed
Italy
March 16th 1918

My dearest Babykins –

I received your sweet letter written Feb. 15 yesterday. You talk awful blue and lonesome my dear and I do wish you would stop worrying and fretting yourself so unecessarily (*sic*) about me. Just because I'm away now is no sign I'll be away all the time and I'm perfectly safe and will be so for some time to come, so why worry? Try to cheer up dear and chase out and enjoy life a little. Dont stick at home and look for trouble. Hear?

MARCH 16, 1918

Mother Rollins writes me some terrible tales about what all you do at home and I dont like it a bit. But what can I do? I warned you not to try to trot around behind Mother all the time. Haven't you found out yet that she can't be happy unless she has fired Ella, Zeke and all the rest and is trying to run the whole "shebang"? If you cant take life easy at home I wish you'd go to Culpepper a while. Wont you? I'd feel much better.

Life looks much brighter to me now dear since I've gotten my commission. However I haven't started my advance flying training yet and may not for another month. We have quite a lot of fun at times and life is not gloomy at all. Occassionally (*sic*) we have some excitement such as an air raid. The other morning about 2 a.m. the alarm was given and some of the fellows got exited and rushed out with their pyjama tails flying, looking for a hole. My Macon lawyer hiked out and tried to get me up too but I was too sleepy and decided I'd wait for the first bomb to get up. He came back in after a little and I was waked up enough to ask if we were going to be bombed. He said "Naw *!@--?, they didn't even pass over here!" He had jumped into the first hole he found which happened to be the ditch that drains the dish water from the kitchen sinks.

Your card dated Jan 31, and letters dated Feb. 3rd, 6th and one from Dad dated Feb 3rd just came in and I see you were much more cheerful and feeling lots better then than you were on Feb. 15th. Since I am going to register this I can't make it too bulky dear so will write again tomorrow to answer them.

I'm enclosing another draft on the Shreveport Commercial National Bank for $50.00 from the Credito Italiane. Be sure and tell me in at least two different letters when you receive it.

I'm in good spirits and health and am confident my little girl is going to be quite alright so now please cheer up and quit looking for the gloom in every thing dearest. Be good and take bestest care of my two babies. With millions of long – kisses and hugs and all my love

Your Devoted
Paul.

Being good doesn't help if a bad motor over-
heats and catches on fire. There is no escape.

Italy
March 20th 1918

My dearest Babykins –

I'm afraid my last couple of letters weren't as cheerful as
they should have been for you know dear your letter of Feb. 15
was so disconsolate it naturally worried me. It is the latest letter
I have from you altho' I have now received your letters dated
Jan 27th, Feb 3rd and 6th, since I received that one. I also have
received the newspapers dear, and yesterday I got your precious
cable. A cable every once in a while is worth its' expense, isn't
it dear? I think I shall send you one every month or so just on
general principles. Think it's worth it?

Since I have my commission life is very
soft. Naturally my worries over my status and
future in the war cease and now I have only you
to worry about and not much longer to do that,
have I dear? Before I realize it my little girl will be her old
"tomboy" self again, only I guess you'll feel like a real grown
up person. But you'll still be just a little girl for a long time yet.
Dont know if you'll ever grow up. Dad is just kidding you when
he says you're the oldest member of the family.

I dont have a thing to do now-a-days except doll up in

MARCH 20,
1918

my new uniform and regalia, with my "Sam Browne" belt and amuse myself. The weather is balmy and delightful. Soon the vinyards (*sic*) and olive orchards will be budding out and this will be a beautiful country. It will be a wonderful sight to sail over in a plane. Last night Keene (the Texan) and I went down to the opera. You know the Italian people are crazy about opera. They have the most wonderful orchestras and the singers have wonderful voices. I could sit all night listening to an Italian orchestra and voices. In our theatres, while the orchestra plays every one talks, but not so in Italy, they know how to appreciate music and at the first note from the orchestra every one becomes motionless and you can hear a pin drop and they sit and seem to just drink in the wonderful music. Then when the music ceases and a dialogue starts every one begins talking again. Then the Italian language sounds so beautiful when sung. They can slide their g's, purr their r's and coo their o's to perfection.

The Teatro here is a massive unique old thing, with beautiful hand paintings on the plaster wall arches and columns some what in the old Roman style. And you know the whole interior is lined with tier on tier of boxes, no balcony or gallery like our theaters have. Every body of any consequence sits in boxes. Our box cost us aproximately (*sic*) .90 cents. It was entered only through a door in the rear and when we went out to smoke between acts the porter locked the door until we came back. We could only understand a smattering of the singing but we certainly enjoyed it.

My dear, you don't want to pay any attention to most of those newspaper articles on flying. As a rule they are written by people who dont know a thing about it. Stinson is really a good amateur flyer but her newspaper "dope" is "full of prunes". Somebody else down here got a clipping where she said she took up flying to earn enough money to pay for a musical education so she could become a concert singer. That ruined her "rep" as a flyer with the bunch down here. I shouldn't have told you about my first experience with a bad machine, but since then I've been up often with a bad motor. On my cross country my motor went bad while I was crossing a wide bay of the sea and 12,000 ft high. It gave me quite a start, figuring which shore was the closest to make a dive for but I only dropped back to 10,000 ft before my motor picked up and started turning over the required 1300 revolutions per. I covered the remaining 60 miles of my cross country with the motor sputtering and spitting in a most disagreeable manner but it was perfectly safe for I simply kept a possible landing field always in view and handled my machine with extra care. In a case like that the only danger that worries me is that the motor may be over heating and likely to catch fire, for if it should catch fire at that height altho' you pointed the nose straight down and dropped like a bullet you would burn up before you could get down. That is one point about my Caproni that I admire. In the cockpit between the engines, you carry two fire extinguishers with which one of the men can put out any fire immediately and with perfect ease. So in that machine that danger is eliminated. The big, majestic old "Cap" is certainly some machine and I'll surely be proud when I get to flying one in a few more weeks. You should never worry a minute over my flying, dear. I assure you I'm good! (Not meaning to be conceited, but if I dont tell you how good I am who will?) Haven't I passed both the Italian aero club tests and the Italian Military Brevet, and am I not now entitled to wear the Italian gold eagle and the American R.M.A. insignia? And if I wasn't a good flyer do you think I could have passed those tests? There's only been a small percentage of fellows down here who failed to make good, but never the less every body didn't. This record was due to the care they used in selecting this bunch from the ground schools. And when I'm in the air you can just bet that I know precisely when I've got a margin of safety and when I'm taking an unusual risk and you'll never know of me taking any chances that are not necessary in the performance of my duty. So many of the younger men delight in taking chances just for the thrills, but not your "old Uncle Dud". I take 'em when I have to only.

I'll mention again dear that I registered you two letters containing a $100.00 draft and a $50.00 draft so you'll be looking for them if you haven't already gotten them. And dearest, I insist that we owe Bill $25. instead of $15. but dont you pay him for I don't want him to spend it yet awhile and I'll send him a draft before long. See, when I come home Bill and I will probably impose on you to the extent of a camping trip, after you and I and our "family" get settled. I have all confidence now in every thing coming out right, so you mustn't worry pet. Be good. I cant tell you what a wonderful girl wife I think I have and how proud of you I am and how I love you. With a million long – soul kisses and hugs and all my love

Your Devoted Paul.

March 25th '18
Italy.

My dearest Babykins –

Just a short note today to tell you the news. I got a letter from our Mother Rollins yesterday, telling me you all had given up going to Monroe. Now Babykins I hope you do which ever you desire for it's alright with me. You know any thing you want to do now is perfectly alright with me, just to show you how you have your husband hypnotized. Of course tho' dearest I'd rather have you at home with your Mother Potts. I'm very proud of you dear for just walking right into Dad's and Mother's hearts like you have done and I know you're the only girl in the world who could do it. But dear I'm afraid you'll over do your self with your incubator and garden and knitting etc. Please be careful darling how you fuss around sitting up nights to regulate your incubator and such. If I had been there I'd have spanked you and put you to bed. You need some body to watch over you all the time dont you. I'll have to come and do it soon. I'd cheerfully give an arm or leg to be with you now.

But to the news, things look very hopeful to me now darling. As you see in the papers the Huns are making their last punch and altho' they may gain a few miles of ground their cause is hopeless for they can't gain enough to do any good. They are on their last legs so cheer up dearest for I (*sic*) be

MARCH 25, 1918

home before you know it and the war will be over.

You know I told you I had applied to get a Caproni sweetheart and up until yesterday I thought I was. But yesterday I was assigned to fly a Sia. (S.I.A.) I can fly any of them, but I just liked the Caproni machine better. However yesterday I went out and took a short flight in a S.I.A. It is extremely fast and handles very sensitively, that is the least movement of the controls brings a quick response. Also it is a terribly high powered little thing, you can point her nose to the sky and go up like a shot. I'll only be here now for a few weeks or a month before I'll go to France to get a few more finishing touches and then this summer I'll be ready for business with brother Hun. I'll take one or two flights a day in the S.I.A. now every good flying day but when I go back to France I'll fly a different machine, still faster and better.

Yesterday my active service orders came sweetheart and now I'm getting my 1st Lieuts. pay plus ten per extra. So in a month now I'll be sending you some more money. Before long I'll be expecting a splendid little cable letting me know my precious wife is alright again and making me very, very, happy. You may have already sent it dear by the time you get this. I have every confidence in your being alright now darling. So you had better be alright. You hear? Now be good. I (*sic*) well and cheerful and very glad to be flying regularly again so don't waste a bit of worry.

With a million long – kisses for my two babies and all my love

Your Devoted
Paul.

❪ GEE! BUT I FELT FUNNY ❫

LaGuardia determined not to use the S.I.A.s after several fatal accidents turned out to have been due to mechanical failure of that airplane.

March 30th 1918
Italy.

My darling babykins –

Yesterday I received your box with the sox, helmet and Prince Albert. I like those sox and the helmet is the best one I have and dear the Prince Albert just got here in time for I was almost out entirely. You mustn't send me any more clothes honey for I have almost more than I can take care of now and wont be able to wear any thing but the lightest and coolest for the warm spring weather is here to stay now dear and I may not be here next winter. You spoke of sending handkerchiefs but my dearest you forget that Italy is a civilized country and I live on the outskirts of a town of 40,000 inhabitants and can go in any time. Whenever you can send anything be sure and put in a dozen or so packs of "Camel" or "Picayune" cigarettes and a few cans of "Prince Albert". Tobacco is the precious article over here darling for I simply cant smoke Italian pipe tobacco in my pipe and the Italian cigarettes are almost as rotten. So precious you mustn't forget that I cant wear knitted goods here in summer and that the

MARCH 30,
1918

main thing I need is cigarettes and tobacco. I still have plenty of cigars left thanks to you, pet, for I'm using them very sparingly.

I also got your two dear letters of Feb. 9 and 11th. No I didn't know any of the fellows on the *Tuscania* but Capt. John Ewing, "Twists" Ewing's brother who was at V.M.I. with me, and he was on a different boat.

So Dr. Bath makes you mad when he insists on seeing you? Well honey dont you know he is working for our own interests when he does? I hope he routes you out every time he comes, you sweet rascal.

I'm glad you sent the letter to the War Risk Ins. Bureau for I've tried to find out about it over here and cant get any satisfaction. I'm only assured that there is to be no policy for fellows taking out insurance on this side. Course it doesn't seem right that you shouldn't have the policy but I cant get it over here and maybe you can get it over there. In writing them you should give them my rank and organization so that they can look me up on the records. 1st Lieut. Aviation Section, Signal Officers Reserve Corps, and I'm stationed at the 8th Aviation Instruction Center American Exp. Forces, Italy. It seems to me that in time you should be able to get a policy from over there. But my hands are tied over here. You see the object of this insurance is to do away with pensions.

Can you beat it? As I was writing the mail orderly came in with your letter written March 2nd which is real recent. I'm relieved to know dear that you got a reply from the War Risk that shows they have the records all O.K. It's alright now my dear, and you'll get the policy from that side. They are so much more efficient in the clerical offices at home than this bunch over here.

I was awful glad to get Bill's pictures but why didn't you send some too? You are so stingy with your good looks. Old Bill is surely beginning to look like a "tony" young scout. Why he'll be wanting to go into long trousers the first thing we know. I'm glad to see him looking so well. That "dorg" looks just like an Italian pup we had here. The "doc" said it wouldn't be sanitary to have him around the place in summer time tho and so made us give him to some Englishmen in a rest camp on the other side of town who haven't quite such rigid ideas about sanitation.

Just as you predicted sweetheart the time has slipped up on me before I quite realized and now when you get this there'll be two babies instead of my one. You'll always be the biggest baby in my family, and that's what I want you to stay. Since so many cheerful confident letters from you and mother I'm sure everything is going to be alright and now I'll be looking for a cable. When that comes then I wont have a thing in the world to worry about except my two babies getting lonesome for their Daddy. I get just as lonesome but I can't tell you about it. But sweetheart I do wish you wouldn't worry so much about my being away at this time. Try to look forward more to the time when I will be home darling, for that I will be home is assured. You haven't anything to worry over about me dearest.

Your letter of Feb. 27 just came also dearest. Maybe I'll get some more before the day is out.

I got Dad's letter and answered it a few days ago. Tomorrow, Easter Sunday, I'll write to Mother and Billie. I have some more news for you sweetheart. The new machine I told you I had started flying has been condemned and so I dont fly it any more you bet. Gee! But I felt funny after I had been flying it so confidently when it was proved to be extremely unsafe. The proving cost quite a price to (*sic*) but I cant tell you what it was. I may go to France soon dear to train on a new machine and I may stay here and fly a "Cap". I don't know which but I'm bubling (*sic*) with health and spirits and I'm confident my two babies are going to be just as alright as if I were there. So darling cheer up and be good. With a million kisses and hugs for my two babies and all my love

Your Devoted Paul.

(over)

Didn't I ever tell you sweetheart, that I got quite a good outfit in New York? You really didn't think I had been living out of the two suit cases I had when you saw me off? I now have an army locker trunk, a bedding roll, a duffle bag and complete officer's equipment. Had to get them and they've certainly paid for themselves. So you see darling I'm fixed <u>quite</u> comfortable, either traveling or in camp. So now be good.

April 2nd 1918.
Italy.

Darling Babykins:-

You know I told you in my last letter a couple of days ago that I had gotten your sweet letters of Feb 10th, 12th and 27th and Mar. 2nd. Letters like those, so cheerful and confident leave me feeling very cheerful and confident myself, even tho' I dont get any more letters for a couple of weeks.

You certainly tickle me sweetheart with your incubator and garden and housekeeping. I never had any idea you'd be such a wonderful little housekeeper. Didn't think you'd like it. But you make me very proud of you and when I come home to you I'll show you. I guess the newspapers are yelling their heads off about this Dutch drive and their long range "pop gun" shelling Paris but dont you believe them. It doesn't make any difference if the Dutch do gain a few miles they can't win now. It's a physical impossibility. And the war cant go on much longer. Every body over here except us are sick to death of it. It will all stop unexpectedly and before you know it I'll be on my way home to you. I hate like thunder to sit around down here all summer tho' with that wonderful scrap going on up in France. It seems a shame that it will be at least four months before I can see actual fighting.

I told you didn't I dear that I had stopped flying a S.I.A.

APRIL 2, 1918

and was again waiting for a Caproni. That is the machine of my choice and now maybe in about a month I'll get assigned to one to fly if they dont run short of men to fly the French machines and send me up there in the meantime.

I'm very anxious for that cable darling altho' I'm confident that you'll come out alright for you remember what you promised me. When you get this I guess the new member will be cutting me out with his wiles, just beating my time completely. Are you going to let a youngster like that knock my nose out of joint? I'd give anything in the world to be with you both darling and I dont know how I'm going to wait until the war is over to see it. I certainly think we both are doing our bit, dont you? Sometimes I almost wish I had been a slacker and waited to be drafted for then I would have been with my wife and baby all this time. But my dear my conscious (*sic*) would have hurt me. Darn the fellow who hangs back and has to be made to fight. I haven't any use for him. A scrap is a scrap and I cant see how any body can sit back merely be an onlooker in a real one. What's hurting me now is that I'm missing the best scrapping opportunity this spring of the whole show. And if it hadn't been for this "stalling" and "bickering" and "delay" over details such as commissions & wasted time from flying I would have been in it. Dont think I'm getting "red eyed" and "blood thirsty" and forgetting what I promised my two babies. No my sweetheart I keep them in mind always and shall look out for their interest but I came over here to fight a war and I'm getting sore now because they dont let me fight. With good luck tho I'll get in it this fall and next summer I'll come home to my babies. I'll have a furlough coming then any way dearest.

Of all the war brides I'm sure none of them can compare to mine darling. I think I knew what a wonderful and sweet one you'd be was why I was willing to make you one. If it hadn't been you what would I have done. Now with the little aviator I'm hoping my biggest, bestest baby wont be so lonesome, and will be able to use up all her surplus love until I come home.

—

Today I've stopped my lazy indolent life and now have plenty to do from 5 A.M. on, however I still have plenty of spare time too. Have to be O.D. and look after hangar and gas details. I'm all eyes for that cable darling. Be real good. With a million – kisses and hugs and all my love to my two babies

Your Devoted
Paul.

World War I-era planes: the Farman biplane (top) and the
French Nieuport biplane (bottom)

World War I-era planes: the Italian Caproni triplane (top) and the Italian S.I.A. biplane (bottom)

April 6th 1918.
Italy.

My dearest Babykins:-

The mail seems to be held up for a while and I'm anxiously looking for a letter and a cable. It is a very inopportune time to me for the mail to stop coming through but I have to indure (*sic*) it.

It is really a good thing that I'm kept pretty busy these days and don't have so much time to sit around and think. Day before yesterday I was Officer of the Day and had to make inspections and check roll calls and I had a lot of fun. I acted like I was going to be very strict and penalize every delinquent very severely and that's where I had my fun, watching the fellows jump around when they saw me coming. I wouldn't have penalized anyone for lots.

It looks like now I may be assigned to a Caproni in a couple more weeks and I'm looking forward to it with a good deal of pleasure. You know for a fellow to really enjoy flying he has to have absolute confidence in his machine and that old machine is certainly a wonder. I'll put my faith in it any day. When you compare piloting a "Cap" and a scout machine it's just like comparing the ocean liner with a gasoline launch. I'm strong for my "air" liner.

APRIL 6,
1918

So Lev McCook transferred to the quartermaster department? It's a pity he didn't wait until he had a chance to try flying for you never can tell whether a fellow has it in him to make a good flyer or not until he takes a machine up and tries it. How did Horace Hughes come out, do you know?

Most people who have never been up in a machine think that the altitude will make them dizzy, but I've never yet been dizzy or even thought of it in a machine and I've floated up around 15,000 ft. but we have a tower here about 150 ft. high and I climbed up the ladder to it's top the other day and got so dizzy I couldnt (*sic*) see straight.

By the way dear I was just about to forget the most important event that has happened lately. Yesterday we received a visit from a real live, living king. The ruling King of Italy. He was a small dapper little man with a very pleasant smile and manner. Of course he was attended by a swarm of generals and staff officers of the Italian army but he didn't seem to be bothered by them in the least, and his visit was received quite naturally, no "jazz bands" or bowing and scraping. He spoke English quite fluently, but with an accent. However I'm not going to tell you a lot of stuff about, "An' sez he to me, sez he" and "Then I says to him, sez I" for I didn't talk to him personally. I was merely one of a group of other flying officers who saluted him and had him pass a few general remarks as he went by. It was amusing to see cameras peeping out of every knot hole and some were brazen enough to run ahead of him and snap him as he went by. He didn't seem to mind tho'.

I'm constantly thinking of my babies and their garden and chickens and all, but I guess my big baby is too busy with her own chick to be doing much else but look after it now. I'm longing now to get back and look after both of you. I dont think it's going to be so awful long now before I do. And dear dont forget your promises to take the very best care of No. 1. baby until then. Hear? Dont forget for one instant how very

very much you two babies mean to me and that I'm thinking of you and loving you every instant. I have to go get busy seeing that the old "Caps" are filled with gas. Be good. With a million long – kisses and hugs and all my love

Your Devoted
Paul

Am enclosing two more pictures of Rome. A picture of St. Peters Cathedral, you can notice it's (*sic*) size by the relative smallness of the people walking up the steps. The other is a view taken from one of the balconies of the Vatican.

119

Pauline Potts, the first child of Paul and Shirley, was born in Natchitoches, Louisiana on April 16, 1918.

Italy
April 20th 1918

My darling Babykins –

Your sweet message which I received yesterday certainly took a load off my mind. Didn't realize just how worried I was dearest until I got that. I wish dear that I could tell you all I feel and think now in an answer but you'll have to wait until I come home.

APRIL 20, 1918

I'm just as proud of my two babies as it is possible for one human to be and there are a thousand things I'd like to ask and as many more I'd like to tell you. I feel so "chesty" over having such a little wife and daughter that I can't help strutting some now. Altho' it is a rainy day today, it looks very rosy to me. How much I'd have given darling to have been home during the past month and now! But we'll make up for it dear when I do come. Wont we?

Now I'm hoping that you wont have such spells of lonesomeness any more and will be happier waiting for me to come back. From now on I guess you'll be a very, very, busy little babykins without me to help you.

Day before yesterday I got your cable saying that you had received the draft and when I first got it I was all keyed up for other news. But after I had read it I was very glad you had sent it for it made me feel that you were alright up to date. You only mentioned a <u>draft</u>, but I suppose you got them both as they were both mailed close together. Thank you sweetheart for being so sweet and thoughtful of me.

When you get this letter about a month from today Miss Pauline will be quite a lady I suppose. I certainly do think this war came at an inopportune time dearest for by all laws of man and nature I should be with you all now. At least where I could come and see you every once in a while. But this old war just rolls merrily on and we have to stick it out to a finish in spite of everything.

Listen here dearest, did you know you had laid the way for a good controversy? Whatever made you call that young lady Pauline when it should have been Shirley? I think Shirley is the most beautiful name and just had my heart set on it. But you're the boss sweetheart and of course you can make it officially whichever you want but in private I'm going to call her Shirley. What does she look like? And how big is she? And can she say Daddy and Mother yet? I know she's going to be the image of her beautiful little mother. You must tell me all about her and my other Babykins too.

Yesterday dearest I also got your two letters of Mar. 13 and Mar. 25 which are the first I've had for two weeks. Will's letter telling me about getting caught speeding also came and I had to laugh at him altho' I know about the time Dad found out about it, it looked like a tragedy in his young eyes. Poor old boy, I'll bet he was scared. And I'll bet he drives slower in town now.

I've started flying again dearest but now I'm perfectly happy at it for I'm flying the very best old "boat" in the world, the same that I wrote you I had applied for and was so in hopes of getting. Gracious but it's a wonderful machine. I'm just in love with it, it's so dependable and trustworthy. Not tricky at all. And you can do any thing in it with perfect safety. Its so enormous in size that I feel like I'm sitting in the cab of a locomotive when I take her off the ground and it keeps you busier than a one-armed paper-hanger, juggling the maize of gas, air and pressure leavers etc., but it is the most enjoyable machine to fly I was ever in. I don't know just how long it will take me to train on it but I'll be here for several months yet darling. Don't you worry about my being on the front any time soon for that will be a long time off.

I have to locally censor my own letters now sweetheart and I'm honor bound not to put any information of value to the enemy in them. But of course the base censor censors them also. So dearest I cant tell you much about my doings. I'm enclosing a picture for you and baby. No it's not a picture of the Commander of the American Forces in Italy. No, wrong again he's not the chief of air service. I'll have to tell you who he is. He's only a flying 1st Lt. otherwise "Daddy".

I'm so full of joy sweetheart that I cant write much today. I wish I could know that my two babies were as happy. Be good, both of you. and kiss each other many many times for Daddy.

With a million long-kisses and hugs and all my love

Your Devoted Paul.

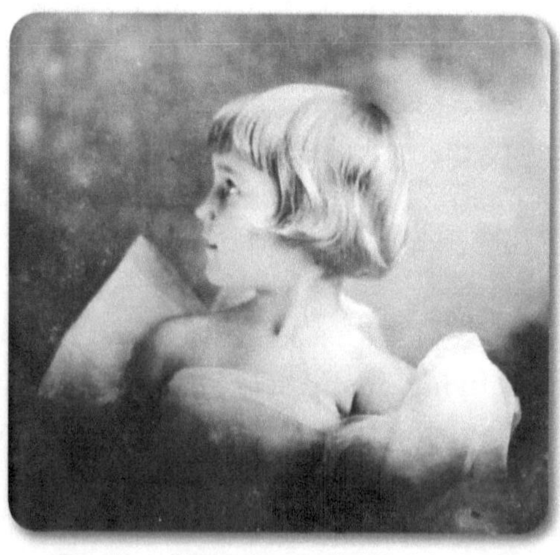

Pauline Potts, born April 16, 1918

—

April 22, '18
Italy

Dear Mother Rollins-

I haven't written you for several weeks now but I'm hoping you'll be lenient in judgement for you can understand how I've been almost worried to death waiting for news from our little girl.

Now I'm so proud of my girl, my two girls in fact, that I know I must bore my associates to death for I cant help strutting around all puffed up like a turkey gobbler. This being a "Daddy" is quite a large feeling.

I think this war is a most inopportune proceeding for now it is going to keep me away from my wife and family for at least the next half year and now of all times I do want to be home. However it has to be gone through with and now I can start with renewed "pep" and energy to do my best.

APRIL 22, 1918

I'm locally censoring my own letters now and so am on honor not to give out any information in them concerning the war lest they fall into the hands of enemy agents so I cant tell you anything about my future moves or flying. But I can say that I'm now flying the best machine made in my estimation and am in love with it. It increases my safety and you all needn't worry about my being on the front anytime in the next several months. I'm crazy to get there for that's what I came over here

123

to do and it's hard to have all this splendid fighting going on
so near and not be able to get in it. Although I have lots to do
nowadays and quite a bit of flying I am more comfortably fixed
and have no hardships.

The girl has been writing some awfully blue letters during
the past month and now I'm expecting them to grow more
cheerful since she has some one else to think of too. I think
she is the bravest girl in the world but I'm afraid she misses her
fun. She likes to be jolly I know, and Mother Potts takes life too
seriously, and she has often wrote me that she was hungry for
your fun so I hope you'll make your letters as cheerful to her as
possible.

The weather and country about here is most beautiful now.
The orchards and vineyards are beginning to show green and
it is certainly a beautiful sight when viewed from high above.
Wish you could all come over and let me take you for a ride in
my new machine.

From the cable I received from my young daughter I judge
she has been officially titled "Pauline" and it almost broke my
heart for I just had it set on "Shirley".

By the time this reaches you I'm sure you'll be back home
and I want to tell you that it was a great comfort to me as well
as my girl for you to be with her.

I'm well and doing fine in my work.

Love
Paul.

April 27th 1918
8th Aviation Instr. Center

My darling Babykins –

Haven't had a letter from you now for at least two weeks it seems and I'm so anxious to get my letters I don't know what to do, especially since I got the dear little cable from little Shirley. How are my two babies today I wonder? Well and happy with each other?

APRIL 27, 1918

I cant tell you, sweetheart, how much better I feel now, how much more pleasure I can get out of my flying and daily life over here, since my anxiety for you has been relieved. Somehow I just knew you would be alright but it took an enormous load off my mind when I got word that you positively were alright. Since I've been over here so long I'm afraid you may forget a little just how very important you are to me. With all your talk of a war garden chickens and incubator, I'm afraid you'll be inclined to neglect your own little self, especially for baby and you know I simply cant countenance any thing like that. You can just bet you'll sure catch it when I come home if I find you've been neglecting those good looks even the least little bit. I'd never forgive you. Hear me?

You said you had already taken me some pictures dearest, to show how fat you are now and were going to take me some

---

more of my two babies together. I'm anxiously looking for them darling so dont delay. I know you all dont realize how much letters and pictures mean to us exiles over here. I'm enclosing a picture of Daddy for his two babies. He had just come down from a successful flight in the old "cap", got away with a good take off, some fairly tight spirals and a good landing so that explains his self satisfied smile. A couple of days before that he came down from a flight and his smile was rather sick and weak and his complexion not quite so dark. Another fellow was driving and he said "Watch me cock her up in a tight spiral", when we were not over 200 meters high. The pilots, there are two, sit side by side and by shouting in each other's ears they can talk. Well, he "cocked her up" at about an eighty degree angle and we started whirling round and round nice and easy when a puff of wind caught the upper wing on the under side and bowled us right over almost upside down. It would have been alright if we had been a thousand meters up instead of only about 200 for it is perfectly easy to correct a position like that by throwing the machine into a dive and then pulling up out of the dive but you will fall and dive down at least 200 meters before you can pull up and get level again. I peeped up at the ground (we were over a field of wheat) and saw one stalk of wheat, then felt a "bottom dropped out" feeling in my "stummick" (*sic*) as the fellow driving forced us back to a vertical banked position and we started dropping sideways (a sideslip), and I could see two stalks of wheat, then three. Just as a picture of the happy home I was leaving behind came before my eyes he got us straightened out by some hook or crook and some cool maneuvering and we had collected so much excess speed that we "zummed" (*sic*) straight up. When he had pushed her over level again he looked over and let out a sigh and gave a sort of sick grin. By a great effort I mustered up a very weak one also. Then he let go of his controls and shouted "you take us home". So I very, very carefully turned around and beat it back to camp and landed like a thistle. I was scared for two days afterwards and believe me I wont do any more spirals after this unless I'm at least 600 meters off the ground. It was real funny after we got down. Still I guess its little tricks like that which happen to every body once in a while that makes flying so fascinating.

Write me just as often as possible sweetheart and tell me everything about my two babies. Dont worry a bit about me, for the weather and life here are fine now. I'm very comfortably fixed and as happy as I can be without you two. So be good and kiss each other many times for Daddy. With a million long-kisses and hugs and all my love

Your Paulie.

1st Lt. P. M. Potts Jr. A.S.S.C.U. A.E.
8th Aviation Instruction Center
American E. F.

❦ "GANG AFT A'GLEY" ❦

8th Aviation Instr. Center
American E. F.
May 9th 1918

My dearest Babykins-
Yesterday and the day before I just received your letters of April 2nd, 3rd and 8th. They were the first I had received for some time dearest and until I got them I was beginning to feel pretty glum.

I didn't know my little girl had been so sick but since I got the cable I'm hoping that you are getting healthy and strong again as I remember you last precious. Yes I'm sure if I could have been with you dear you wouldn't have been sick at all, I just wouldn't have let you. You must hurry up those pictures dear so I can see for myself how you are now.

I cant help but laugh at you and your chickens and incubators. Who would have thought sweetheart that you would have turned into such a farmer. Don't you care tho' if those eggs wouldn't hatch, I know if they wouldn't for you they wouldn't for any body else. Personally I just think you did fine with them. Wish you wouldn't think so much of putting mother to trouble dear. You don't put her to any trouble. She needed a daughter just as Billie did a sister. Wish you'd settle down at home honey and stop worrying about troubling any body. You are too sweet to

MAY 9,
1918

128

be a bother even if you tried. I know.

When I left home so long ago to come over here we thought I'd be back with you again by now didn't we sweetheart? "The best laid plans of mice and men gang aft a'gley" however sweetheart and you and our little Shirley will just have to be brave as <u>you</u> have been for a little while longer at least sweetheart. No one can say how much longer this war is going to last but I can't see how human endurance is going to last many more years. I'm heartily sick and tired of it babykins. But you mustn't worry a moment babykins for I'm perfectly alright here and as long as I stay here it is at least fairly certain that I'll come back to my two precious babies at some future date.

The other night the school in town which corresponds to a high school at home, don't know what they call it here, gave a little show in the big theatre here and myself and a couple of other fellows went down with a bunch of Italian officers. The music, as usual, was wonderful and the kids put on a swell show. The little rascals seem to be born actors, and we saw some real talent. Of course all the towns' select proud mothers and fathers were out and it was quite a social affair. We had one of the professors in our box who spoke good English and he interpreted for us. I've gotten so I have a most profound respect for the Italian better class. After you get to understand their customs and the way they are raised, that is kind of understand them, they are splendid. Talk of hospitality, they are truly hospitable. Our noted southern hospitality is crude by the side of theirs. I know we appear boorish in their eyes, we are so crude and rough mannered.

Johnnie Pender's letter was certainly refreshing. I'm going to answer right away and I'm glad Dad wrote and explained that I was over here for it would have taken so long for him to get my letter and he'd have been hurt not to get an answer. He really has done quite well. A "Sub" at old V.M.I. is a big dog for so young a kid. He was too young to get in the army when he finished but I don't think he is now so I'll talk up flying to him. Funny, but my "Macon lawyer" "bunkie" went to France to fly a different type machine and now my bunkie is an older fellow who used to live at Johnnie's home town and knew him as a kid. He is the finest kind of fellow and has a gift for talking "n — talk" which makes me very homesick at times.

I keep very busy now-a-days sweetheart which is really very much better for me than the inactivity of the winter. But, I can never get so busy that I don't think of my two babies every second. Be two real good babies and kiss each other a thousand times for Daddy. With a million long-kisses and hugs and all my love for my two babykins

Your Devoted
Daddy.

1st Lieut. Paul M. Potts Jr. A.S.S.C.USR.
8th Aviation Instruction Center
American E. F.

❧ HOLDING ON TO BRACE WIRES ❧

American E. F.
May 15th 1918

My darling Babykinses-

Just received a splendid bunch of letters from you, Mother Rollins, Mother Potts and Pauline yesterday. There were five of your sweet letters, dated, April 10th, 12th, 15th, 17th and 20th. I got two from Mother Potts dated April 14th and 18th and a short one from Mother Rollins dated April 16th. So dear I certainly wasn't neglected for that period.

Did you get your birthday cable sweetheart? I allowed several days for its' transmission hoping it would come to you on the 11th. Also dearest I wrote a hurried note that day and wished I could write you a long one, but I had a terrible cold and the start of a chill and fever spell and felt worse than I have since I've been over here. The Doc stuffed me full of quinine and a lot of other dope tho' and got me all right again in a couple of days. Now dont you go to imagining that I'm sick or apt to be sick. For I'm not now. We have just as good medical attention down here as could be gotten at home. The greatest inconvenience I found in being sick a couple of days was that I couldn't fly.

I had a good flight this morn tho. Was up over half an hour playing around at low altitudes, 2,000 or 3,000 ft. The air was very calm and smooth so I was able to make some nice

MAY 15,
1918

131

tight smooth spirals etc. but I always have trouble landing. I just can't seem to sit this heavy machine down on the ground properly. It's so heavy and big that it has to be done "just so" every time and I cant do it just as it should be yet. However I find I'm improving right along. A little more practice and I'm sure I'd get to be perfect. Yesterday I had a most uncomfortable ride in the "cock pit" between the side motors. Theres (*sic*) no seat there to strap yourself to and you just kneel down and hold on to the brace wires. The air was terribly rough and we rocked and pitched around like a chip on a stormy sea. It is truly alarming to ride in that old bus when the air is very rough. The two fellows in the pilots seats were strapped tightly to their seats and their attention was taken up with driving so they weren't bothered so much by the sudden jolts and lunges of the machine as we'd hit air pockets and contrary currents. But me, why half the time I was hanging out behind with nothing touching but my death grip on the brace wires. Once we hit a stretch of smooth air and I had just relaxed a little to get a good breath when we came to the end of that smooth current and dropped into a pocket. She just went straight down like a rock for 75 or 100 ft. As the bottom went out from under me I just managed to hook a little finger around a wire to hold on by. When I got my feet planted on the floor of the cock pit I held them there, believe me. When we came down they asked me if I wanted to go up and drive some and I said, "No thanks!" So we waited for smoother weather. It's really lots of fun riding behind some one else. I often do it.

Those letters make me awfully homesick for you and the kiddy, dearest. I'd have given anything in the world to have been with you when you were sick. But never mind sweetheart I'll make up for it after this old war is over. We three will have a wonderful time.

I'll bet that kid is the sweetest thing in the world. I dont see how I'm going to be able to wait very long to see her. Why if this old war lasts very long she wont know she has a daddy.

———

She is going to be some spoiled baby, I'll bet, with a mother like you and two grandmothers and a granddad catering to her all the time. But I dont care. I'll probably spoil her as much as anyone when I come home.

I keep so busy now-a-days sweetheart. I dont have near as much time to write as I use to have. We save so much daylight by going to bed late and getting up so early that whenever I do get a vacant hour in the day I have to use it to keep up with my sleep. When you're flying regularly you must keep up your necessary amount of sleep for it will sure tell in your flying. Makes you nervous and uncertain. So darling if my letters dont come quite so regularly for a while now you'll know I'm doing my best. I'm sticking in another picture for my two babies. You must use the address below dear, for it will get me quicker I think. I haven't gotten the P.A. tobacco from Mother Rollins yet but still have some of yours left. If that new law about parcels (we've heard it was annulled) will allow you please send me some more Prince Albert. Be two very good babies and kiss each other many times for Daddy. With millions of long kisses and hugs and all my love

Your Daddy

1st Lt. Paul M. Potts Jr. A.S.S.C.U.S.R.
8th Aviation Instruction Center
American Exp. F.

Could the "friend" in this letter have been Percy W. "Red" Graham, the redheaded Chicago native who was the most celebrated collegiate athlete of that time? He wasn't named in this letter, but how many redheaded pilots were there in 1918?

May 20th 1918
8th Aviation Instr. Center
American E. F.

My dearest Babykinses –

Received your sweet letter of April 25th today. It had the little newspaper clipping and verse in it you know. Yesterday I got a letter from Margaret telling me how crazy she was to see Pauline and how nicely her (*sic*) and Bud are doing. So you see the postman has been very good to me during the last two weeks.

MAY 20, 1918

I'm so glad dear you were getting alright when you wrote this last letter. But honey you never told me how sick you had been before. If I had known I'd have been worried sick myself. I did know tho' honey that it was going to go very hard for my little girl for who ever heard of such a little delicate trick getting away with a thing like that. I'm so proud of you I dont know what to do with you.

I'm crazy to see those pictures you said you were taking.

And I do hope you'll get some of my big baby too. If you didn't this time then do so right away. The Censors have become very strict about the pictures we send home. Have to be very careful to send nothing but personal ones with no local color in them. I guess you've noticed too that they have become equally strict about how we fix our letters up and what we say. But dont worry dear, if you cant learn about the war now you can when it's over and I come home.

I had a "wild eyed" ride with a red headed "son of Erin" yesterday afternoon* and returned same to him. On account of the direction of the wind we were landing parallel to the buildings of a sheep ranch which stands on one edge of our flying field. I went up as an observer first with my red headed friend driving and he gave me a very enjoyable ride until he came back to camp and cut the motors and started gliding down to a landing. He turned and twisted a bit then trying to get into position to land and lost all his altitude and wound up headed straight for the back door of the little stone ranch house. We were too low and close to it then to bank up and turn back on to the field and I didn't give him credit for having sense enough to put his motors on and go over it so I got all set to land in a soft spot when we should hit. He did tho' and we went up over it and twisted back on to the field with the motors on and he landed us on one wheel and one wing skid. Didn't break anything tho' so then I took him up behind me and did identically the same thing without intending to only, after I dodged the house I landed level and made a couple of bounces out of it like frog leaps. So we "balled" each other out and swore we wouldn't ride together again but this morning it came our turn together again and we both assured each other we'd drive very carefully and be considerate of the feelings of the one who was passenger but we both pulled the wildest spirals imaginable without intending to. You get more thrills riding

*See Notes, page 256

---

with someone else driving then you can imagine. If we didn't know how to fly it would be different, but when you ride in a machine that you know a little about flying the things you think about when someone else is flying you are dreadful. But you get good practice.

These days, flying is not all I have to do, tho' most of the day is spent out on the field. I'm allways (*sic*) fooling with machines, inspecting them etc. and have many other duties. It's really much better for me than the former inactivity tho' for it keeps my mind occupied and makes time pass faster.

Yes sweetheart I have the little medal still and now wear it on my identifycation (*sic*) disk on my wrist. I have a nice little silver disk you know with my name and army address on the outside and my home address on the inside and I have attached the medal to the chain. You know dear I spoke of your sending me some P.A. tobacco in my last letter. Well if you cant send it dont bother for I can get other tobacco over here.

I'm as well and healthy as can be dear and vastly more contented since I know my two babies are doing so well so dont worry a minute. Be two real good babies now. With millions of long – kisses and hugs and all my love and kiss each other a million times for me

Your Paulie.

1st Lt. Paul M. Potts Jr. A.S.S.C.U.S.R
8th Aviation Instruction Center
American Exp. F

———

136

﴾ "BABY CAP" ﴿

You can't write a letter while your co-pilot does spirals.

8th Aviation Instr. Center, American E. F.
May 28, 1918

Dearest Babykinses—

Did I tell you in my last letter that I had your letter of April 29 and Dad's and Billie's letters of April 19th and 27th? I know I haven't written you for a week for I've been just very busy and too tired to write in spare time. I certainly enjoyed those last three letters I mentioned dear, but I'm sure you must have been a little blue and I had thought Pauline wasn't going to let you be blue a minute. <u>You</u> haven't anything to worry over dear, for things are just turning out fine for me.

May 28, 1918

During the past week I have been doing my solo work in the "Baby Cap", that is, the smaller one. It's not what could be called "small" but it's the smallest of them. The "young one" the fellows call it. You know as "Cap" pilots we'll pair off so "Dug" Farquhar and I have duly decided to pair off with each other if the powers that be will allow us. It looks hopeful for when I did my Brevet yesterday in the "young one" he got permission to go up with me. It was the first time we've ever ridden together and it's lots of fun. He wrote a note to his girl on the back of an envelope when we were about 3,000 ft. up. I saw what he was doing and cocked us over into a tight spiral and made him cut it rather short for I dont think anyone will continue writing when that enormous old bus begins grinding around in a spiral. I gave him the controls for a few minutes so as to see how he flew and decided he's pretty good. He calmly shut off a side motor and began evoluting around meantime looking around at me with a grin like, "see what I can do". I got back at him a little. . . (*The censor cut out the description on the other side of the paper, which then interrupted this narrative for a few lines.*)

I like my machine better and better every time I go up in it. It's absolutely the most dependable bus made.

I was very sorry to learn of the death of my old instructor a short while ago at another camp. He was a most likable chap and I had more confidence riding behind him than any one I've flown with since. He was killed in a smash.

(*The censor cut out the next segment, which probably described a different crash, not the deadly crash of Paul's old instructor. This elision also deleted the writing on the other side of the paper (as noted above)*) . . . and came out without a scratch. He got balled up making a landing and his machine turned a flip on the ground. I was there and thought that was the end of him but he came crawling out without a scratch, scared stiff. He's the only one of our old crowd who has even had any kind of a serious smash. The only members of our old ground school bunch left with me are Dug Farquhar, Curt Keen, Norm (?) Sweetser, Letzig and McCain. They often ask me about you. The rest have scattered.

I have to study and bother with a lot of drill now. It seems a flying officer now not only will have to be proficient in all matters pertaining to flying but will have to be a proficient infantry officer also to a certain degree. It doesn't come hard with me tho' for I've had so much experience in the infantry

—

before, you know.

You all are a great pair of kids. I wish I could be with you. Even if one of you does sleep nearly all the time. How can you blame everybody in town for wanting to see Pauline. Surely she is a wonderful girl. Her granddad and grandmothers seem to be tickled to death with her. I cant see how I'm going to wait until the war is over to see her. But what makes you say you have taken a back seat in favor of her? Neither one of you are going to allowed to take any back seat with me.

I'm glad you are sending me some cigarettes for I've been out of them now for a while but my Prince Albert will hold out for a while longer until I get your next batch easily. Will's last letter was very cute. He's getting quite original and writes very interesting letters now. I think he likes Pauline after all. I can't tell you how proud I am of my two babies sweetheart. Kiss each other a thousand times for me and dont worry or be blue about Daddy for he's well, happy and doing fine. With a million long kisses and hugs and all my love

Your Devoted Paulie

1st Lieut. Paul M. Potts Jr.
8th Aviation Instruction Center
American Exp. F.

A COUPLE OF CUTE KIDS

8th Aviation Instr. Center

American E. F.

June 1st 1918

My dearest Babykinses:-

Just got your dear letter with the pictures dated May 8th, this morn, and also one on April 28th and May 6. I'll say I have a couple of cute kids! And proud I am. Both of you look as fat as can be. I think you've been getting cuter every day since I've been over here if such a thing is possible. Perhaps Pauline has been having something to do with this. She looks like a little rolly polly to me, utterly satisfied with life. Altho' those pictures make me terribly home sick, they also make me feel better and in closer touch with my "couple a kids". So take some more and send me every once in a while sweetheart.

Yes I can plainly see "that garden" in one of them. I think you are the most wonderful girl to accomplish so much. There's no question in my mind dear as to whether I have a capable wife or not. I'll say I have.

JUNE 1, 1918

You tickle me sweetheart, talking about your "pep" and declaring yourself. I'm glad you have some left and are going to use it. I want you to.

I wish you had kept Victorine longer dear. I know you will have let her go while you still needed her, but I had no way of telling you to keep her as long as she was the slightest use to you unless I had cabled and then it would have been too late.

I'm afraid you're getting like a miser and I dont want you to be that way where you and Pauline are conscerned (*sic*). In my next letter I'll send you a draft for $50.00 and after that can send a larger amount every month without hurting myself.

I'm enclosing a postcard picture. I had to have one taken to paste on my identification card and the photografia wouldn't print less than six. So I'll burden you and the entire family with one. Dont think I'm as sad as that looks, for that picture was taken at one of my gloomiest moments. The Italians are great posers and take pictures seriously and he had just been posing me for 30 minutes, and telling me things I couldn't comprehend so my patience was about gone. Now both of you be as sweet as you look in those pictures and kiss each other a thousand times. With millions of long kisses and hugs and all my love

Your Devoted
Paulie.

1st Lt. Paul M. Potts Jr.
8th Aviation Instruction Center
American Exp. F.

§ THE 4:15 A.M. WHISTLE §

8th Aviation Instr. Center
American E. F.
June 13th 1918

My dearest Babykinses:-

JUNE 13,
1918

I have your letters of May 9th, 12th and 17th with the last set of pictures which are just too sweet for words. I cant see much difference in the young Pauline but you are looking better. I'm just about ready to puff up and burst with pride in my two kids. I'd have loved to have had a peep at you in the Red Cross Parade for I know without seeing it you were the best looking pair of babies in it but of course if I had been there you wouldn't have been in it. I cant see from the pictures tho' why everyone says Pauline looks like me for it seems to me she favors you more. I think she looks just like that baby picture I had of you.

You tickle me when you go to talking like you think you are getting old and staid with a family. You are just as much a baby as Pauline is so where do you get that talk? In your Mother's last letter she noticed it too and I told her it wouldn't take me any time to get it out of your little head as soon as I got home. Think so?

Dont worry about the tobacco dear. There seems to be a rumor that we're going to be able to get American tobacco down here some time. In fact about a month ago the Y.M.C.A.

issued each of us eight packs of cigarettes, sixteen in a pack. Mine lasted me two weeks. They may let us have some more. The tobacco in France doesn't do us much good for we cant get a pinch of it. However a fellow who left here had quite a supply of Prince Albert and he let me have half a dozen cans, which, added to what I had will last me for two months. Then Mother Rollins wrote that her package of P.A. had not been returned to her so it must have gotten through. Anyway I'll wait a month to see what turns up before I send you an order.

Also dearest I'm enclosing a draft for $50.00 in this letter. If you need more please let me know. If I can ever get myself a complete outfit I'll be able to send you more. You know the bill passed to pay us our extra pay for flying but they pay no attention to that over here and we only get a straight lieutenants salary when we are flying day in and day out. Some one seems to have the idea that we love to fly so well that we'd almost be willing to pay the government for the use of the machines. Our outfit and clothes costs us more than that for other branches and our living expenses are much higher so that we downright need the money, at least those of us who have others to think of. I dont think we are getting just treatment along those lines, but perhaps it will be straightened out at some future time. However sweetheart that is no reason why you should do away with baby's nurse and washwoman. The ridiculous price you get them for is nothing. The comfort I get from knowing you have them is worth much more. And sweetheart if you dont get both back immediately I'll be miserable. I dont want you looking like you are 40 yrs. old when I come home, I'd turn right around and leave again. And if you dont take care of yourself you'll be looking just that way. You cant take care of Pauline without assistance and what money I send you is for just such things as that. So please dear dont try to economize that way. Will you be good now?

I hope you will by all means go to see Mary for a while. It will be a diversion for you sweetheart. Your Mother wrote, she would go with you just to get you to go. When you do give my best to Mary.

I'm writing this at 6 a.m. sitting right out under the open sky. We are all having a fresh air cure thrust on us. The whistle blows at 4:15 a.m. (the worst horror of the whole war) and whether you are going to fly or not and no matter how late you were up the night before, out of bed and out of barracks you go and by Doc's orders we have to stay out for three hours, to get fresh air and wake up thoroughly. It's terrible! Some of us are getting to be experts at the art of arrangining (*sic*) ourselves over the back of a chair and catching up a little sleep that way. Me, for the quieter life of the front line trenches!

Be two real sweet girls now and kiss each other many times for Daddy. With a million long kisses and hugs and all my love

Your Devoted
Paulie

O.K.
Paul M. Potts Jr.
1st Lt. A.S.Sig. R.C.
8th Aviation Instruction Center
American Exp. F.

❦ AN AXLE BROKE ON LANDING ❧

8th Aviation Instr. Center
American E. F.
June 20th 1918

My darling Babykinses-

I'm again living an easy life comparatively speaking and enjoying it so hugely that I'm going to endeavor to write you a cheerful letter, for cheerful is my mood now. The main and only factor in my easy life is that the Doc has repented and at last decided that it is really not necessary to our health for us to get up at 4:15 A.M. After long deliberation he has decided that we may be almost as healthy if we don't get up until seven. So except when I have duties that require me to be up at 4:15 I can now sleep till seven!

Curt Keen, the tall boy from West Texas you remember, and I flew together nearly all day yesterday and completed our brevetto or test in "the large machine". "Capite?" We spiraled and played around at 10,000 ft. for about 50 minutes having a most enjoyable time. We purposely didn't go much over 10,000 for it began to get rather painfully cold above that. We took turns flying the machine and also making the take offs and landings. Curt is a real good flyer but I beat him spiraling. It fell to me to make the landing as we came in on the last ride and the sun was down and it was getting pretty dusky and hazy on the ground so I was being particularly careful, especially as one

JUNE 20, 1918

of the axles on the landing wheels was weak and partly bent. I was landing with a tail wind, that is the wind was blowing in the same direction I was going, and that makes you land with twice as much speed as you do landing head into the wind as you should. I didn't want to land that way but two machines going in just ahead of me were landing that way so I had to land the same way too. We made a velvety smooth landing going about 90 miles and rolled for a quarter mile across the field. Just as we had almost stopped the weak axle gave way and bang, crash! the right wing went down on the ground. We had slowed up so much that it didn't do very much damage but if it had given way a second sooner before we lost our excess speed, Curt and I and the fellow who was riding as passenger with us, not to mention the machine, would surely have been strewn about in various places all over that field. It's customary for the chief pilot to say something very sarcastic and cutting to a pilot when he smashes, provided the pilot is in fit condition to be talked to, and while Curt and I were looking it over he came taxying (*sic*) up in another machine. We thought we were in for a "balling out" but he only laughed at us and told us we were lucky. So we felt alright.

We dont seem to be going to pair off the way we wanted too (*sic*). Dug is farther along on the list then either of us and is paired off by the authorities with another fellow. Then Curt and I were going to be paired together by the authorities but he is going to be held for an instructor in primary training so now I'm paired officially with a fellow named Forsythe. He is a very nice fellow, quiet and likeable and has seen eight months service in the American Ambulance corp (*sic*) up in France before he got into aviation. I've flown with him and he's good, very steady and cool, so I'm still very well satisfied. Just so you have a pardner (*sic*) you have confidence in.

Did you get the other letter with the $50 draft in it? Dont forget it's to use when you need it. I want my two babies to be comfortable while I'm away. Now be good and dont worry

—

about me a bit for I'm alright and cheerful as can be. I'll begin
night flying soon. With a million long – kisses and hugs and all
my love.

Your Devoted
Paulie

O.K.
Paul M Potts Jr.
1st Lt. A.S.Sig. R.C.
8th Aviation Instruction Center
American E. F.

Paul's photograph from his Caproni aircraft

❧ INKY BLACKNESS ❦

Night flying required special training and was a
true test of nerves.

8th Aviation Instr. Center, American Exp. F.

June 21st 1918

My dearest Babykinses –

I'm awful anxious now to get a letter of late date from my
little girl as the last ones had been on the way over a month. I
guess I'll get a big bunch of them soon.

JUNE 21, 1918

It's almost a year now since that wonderful
last 14th of July dearest and the war goes right
on regardless. We didn't think or dream it
would last so long then did we dearest? But no
matter how long I'm kept away from my two babies I'll come
back to them finally and we'll make up for all this lost time. So
dont you worry dear. Just take things easy and think of then.

I've been doing some flying at night dearest. Made three
short flights between 2 and 3 a.m. the other night. It was
inky black, no moon and the clouds and mist hid the stars. Of
course I had a night instructor with me. We had a searchlight
to land by and we took off in the beam of its light. For a few
seconds after we left the ground we were still in its' (*sic*) light
but soon we plunged into the inky blackness and positively
honey I couldn't see the nose of the machine, and would not

have been able to see my hands on the controls had it not been for the dim reflection from the stream of fire shooting from the exhausts. I could only see blackness beneath and the little beam of the searchlight way below and behind us was no larger than a pencil. I felt like one of those shooting stars you've seen. How I flew that machine I dont (*sic*) know. I just found that some way or other I could tell when we were tipping over, when we were going up or down and when we were turning. I made some flat wide spirals and decided to come down, so pushed the nose over, cut the motors and just plunged down into the inky black below. It was like closing your eyes and jumping into a well so deep you could not see the bottom. I turned and twisted, losing altitude all the time, waiting for the beam of light to grow "life size" which would tell me if I was near the ground. The instructor turned on the headlights of the machine and we could see its' beam trailing off to nothing in the blackness below. Then the searchlight began to grow rapidly larger and all of a sudden the headlight of the machine struck bottom. So I knew we were close to the ground and put on the motors again and flew over the searchlight, then glided down into its beam where I could see and landed alright. We made two more flights and I had the same sensations, except that once the searchlight went out as I was gliding down and then the instructor took the controls and landed us by the light from our machine's headlight. When our headlight "struck bottom" he leveled the machine, but the ground wasn't there so he pushed over and leveled again a little lower just making a "step down". We felt the ground and then everything was fine again. He told me I'd probably never fly again when it was as black dark as that and I hope so. It's alright when the moon and stars are out for then you can see the ground, the roads, houses and fields and keep your bearings very well. I only have a little more to do and I guess now that it's alright with the Censor for me to tell you of it.

By the way dearest I'm fixed fine for cigarettes now. The

Y.M.C.A. down here has loads of them now. Good ones too and they sell them at the same price as over in the States. So dont worry a bit more about my smokes and be two real good girls and kiss each other many times for Daddy and dont worry for I'm well and contented. With a million long-kisses and all my love

Your Devoted
Paulie

O.K.
Paul M. Potts, Jr.
1st Lt. A.S. Sig. R.C.
8th Aviation Instr Center
American Exp. F.

8th Aviation Instr. Center
American Exp. F.
June 29th 1918

Dearest Babykinses –

For between two and three weeks now I hadn't a letter from you but today the mail man brought me six, dated May 21, 26, 29, June 1, 3 and 5th. I had the dumps something awful for want of a letter from my babies and whether they were all cheerful or not they raise the gloom for the sole reason that they are from my little Shirley.

I certainly do, darling, realize what a very hard time you are having of it and words just cant tell you dearest how sorry I am, how I sympathize and I long to be able to take charge of your troubles and smooth them over but honey I'm helpless. I cant do a thing for you that I can see. If there is a thing no matter what it is that I could write please tell me sweetheart. You'll just have to take up for your own rights. Didn't I tell you ages ago that you'd have to assert yourself? Stand on your own feet and not meekly let any one impose on you?? If you cant be happy in your surroundings then I can send you more money, honey, and you can change them and that's all I can see that I can do, and I'll gladly do that if it will make you any more contented.

I'm glad Mother Rollins will be with you soon – this is the

last of June so I suppose she is with you already – perhaps it will cheer you up some. I dont see tho' why she couldn't stay with you and Pauline instead of in the Club but if she did I dont suppose she'd accomplish much. You two would surely keep her busy consoling you.

I think Bob and Margaret certainly had the right idea when they advised you to put trouble in the background and put on a grin even if you had to force it. I wish you could see the things I've had to swallow and since there could be no good in wearing a grouch, I grinned, just for my friends sakes I guess for it is much pleasanter to look on a smile than a frown. Then I found that it did me good. When you've flown until your nerves are raw and can almost feel them vibrate and then still have to make another flight and while you are getting your equipment all adjusted your knees want to knock together and your teeth want to chatter do you let your flying partner see it? Sure not! You set your leg muscles to keep your knees steady and screw up your face in a grin. Then if he's all in like you are perhaps your grin and apparent steadiness help settle his nerves. It's seldom I do enough flying in a day to get that way and a rest all ways soothes a fellow and makes him eager to be up again but you do get over dozes. And as for anticipating troubles! Niente! Take every day just as it comes and start your grin working early so as to have the jump on any thing that turns up. Of course sweetheart you'll say this "grin dope" is alright to preach but a different thing to practice but honey I've honestly tried it out and it helped so much that now I keep it up. Basta!

Yes I'm a little thinner, dearest. But I'm still as healthy as they make them. Lack of proper food is the most likely cause for I get neither enough nor decent food. It is simply impossible to obtain it in this particular section because they dont know what it is. Do you know that last fall we used to have snail pies? Have you seen the snails that crawl up on fence posts at home and leave a sticky trail? It is the same variety. They are considered very delicious in this section. I ate the sticky meat pies derived from them several times before I found out what they were. Needless to say I didn't eat any more after I found out what they were. Now we have American cooks but they can only find enough to cook for one meal a day. The other two meals are merely formalities. But I wont be here much longer. Perhaps two weeks, so I can grin a genuine grin over that.

This may sound like complaining, dearest, and it may sound like a sermon but it's neither. I'm just trying to give you a glimmer of our day to day philosophy down here.

My flying partner, Earl Forsythe, is a very jolly likeable fellow, always cheerful. About every third day tho he grows serious and says "O!?......!%#!! I wish this war was over". Then he grins. He says I'm a better pilot than he is but I'm not. He never corrects me in the air or shows any nervousness at all when I'm driving and so I think he has wonderfully steady nerves. I cant help fidgeting in my seat and offering suggestions tho', when I'm not driving, to save me. I must have a very nervous makeup. We get along beautifully tho. The other day when we were up bombing he steered me a perfect line right across the center of the target and enabled me to make two direct hits out of four shots which was very good. But I'll try not to take up this letter with flying dearest. You'll have to forgive me for filling my letters so full of it but just remember that that is all we ever do down here, all we know and all we talk about.

I appreciate every body being so nice to you and Pauline. Think you should bury the hatchet with the Roys and not hold a grudge against them. Dont you dear? Aren't you going to visit Mary? I was anxious for you to go for it would do you good. If it's clothes you want dearest, why, you'll just have to get them yourself. I send you the money sweetheart and have asked you to spend it for what you want and if you need more I can send more, but my dear I cant go down town and buy them myself. And I've asked you to dress well and not pay any attention to hard times talk. Wont you??? And dearest as long as you're home please keep Aunt Liz or someone to assist with Pauline or the thought of your being without assistance will drive me into the hands of the Huns.

No, Dug is not with me any more. He's been gone about two weeks now. He was lucky (?) and got out ahead of me. We were in hopes of going together, but I'll be with him again soon.

I guess you've seen accounts in the papers by now of the doings of the first American, Italian trained, flyers working in the Italian squadrons. The papers over here have mentioned it so I guess it's alright for me to mention it.

You cant tell me too much about that wonderful girl Pauline, sweetheart. Your letters are the only compensation I have for what I'm missing. But dont neglect telling me about your own sweet self. Hear?? And dont forget for an instant what my two babies mean to their Daddy. Be good and never doubt that you are always in my mind and that I'm true. Kiss each other many times for Daddy. With a million long – kisses and hugs and all my love

Your Devoted
Paulie.

O.K.
Paul M. Potts Jr.
1st Lt. A.S.Sig. R.C.

BLACK AS A BLACK CAT
UP A CHIMNEY
or
NERVOUS AS THUNDER

8th Aviation Instr. Center
American Exp. F.
July 7th 1918

Dearest Babykinses:-

Just a short note tonight to send you this $50.00 Am. Exp. Money order I've enclosed and ask you kids how you are? Come sta mia carissima bella signorina? Eh! Yes I'm endeavoring to learn Italian now. "Endeavor" is right. U. Sam issued me an Eyetalian grammar so I presume he meant me to study it and this is the first thing I learned.

Did you get the $50 I sent about June 19th?? Remember sweetheart all I send is for you to use for your comfort so use it freely and if you can use more just let me know. Hear?? I was surprised that I could get this money order right here. Think it is better than the drafts. And Listen Precious I got one for $25.00 for Will which I will send him tomorrow. It's better to send them for small amounts in case any are sunk. If you have paid him $25 already then he can turn it over to you, or the balance of what you have given him.

I hope my kids are cheerful now. As cheerful as I am. Are you? I'm feeling very good tonight in spite of the fact that it's

JULY 7, 1918

black as a black cat up a chimney and I'm going out to fly in about an hour. That explains this scratchy writing. Can you tell I'm nervous as thunder? I often wish I could do my flying at night over there where I could look down like the angels on you kids asleep.*

I haven't properly answered those last six letters sweetheart that I'm afraid I fussed at you about in my last letter a few days ago and if I dont lose too much sleep tonight and tomorrow night a nice fat letter will follow this one. I have a lot to tell you about the big 4th of July banquet and celebration we pulled off. A most tony (Tony) affair. I wished a thousand times you could have been with me so I could have enjoyed it more.*!?$ I wish this war was over!!! Dont you? Really tho' sweetheart I know I shouldn't joke about it. It's too serious a thing to us, but it will be over one of these days before many more moons. Just going to run itself out.

The Y.M.C.A. has just outdone itself dearest and we have (*sic*) now have oodles of good American Cigarettes. So dont worry a bit more about my smokes precious for I now have enough to last me six months.

I'm just doing fine and as well and safe and contented as can be. Kiss each other many times for me love me lots. With all my love and a million kisses and hugs always.

Your Devoted
Paulie.

O.K.
Paul M. Potts Jr.
1st Lt. A.S. Sig. R. C.

* See Notes, page 256

———

156

❦ A "GOLLY" DAY ❧

8th Aviation Instr. Center
American Exp. F.
July 9th 1918

Darling Babykinses-

I wanted to write you yesterday but after being up all night couldn't manage anything but a letter to Billie. Now I've sent you a $50 money order on the 7th and a $25 one for Bill on the 8th. Be sure and mention when you get them.

I wish you could have seen the "blow out" and "tea fight" we had on the 4th dearest. It was a "golly" day. In the morning we went down to the city square where all the generals, big pistols and politicians in this part of the country were assembled prepared to toot first their horn and then ours before the assembled Italian multitude. And since you've never seen an Italian multitude you cant imagine anything like it. It's a masterpiece in multitudes. There we stood, first on one foot and then the other for infinity, while the bally-hoo men on the speakers (*sic*) platform foamed and snorted. At last the smoke and fireworks were over and the mayor of the town took us horsifers (officers) up to his palatial mayors mansion and fed us ice cream and cookies and all to the pleasing accompaniment of popping champagne corks. We had a rest period then until 4 P.M. when our "tea fight" started. The Italians had decorated a large empty hangar for us and did the most wonderful job of decorating I ever saw. All the notables and elect? (elite) families were there in full force and we fed them tea and cakes (camouflage) and afterwards ice cream etc. and in order to make the toasts a success champagne. We also showed them moving pictures of ourselves. As an afterthought it occurs to me that either the champagne cost a great deal more than the tea or there was a great deal more champagne than tea, one of the two. You know in Italy, Italians wouldn't think of a meal (even breakfast) or a party without wine or champagne. If they could only have one of the two then rest assured it wouldn't be the meal. Well our tea party was quite a success and at seven we went into town and followed a band around some of the principal streets while the worshiping populace threw showers of roses and imitation flowers in our path. Yes, it was quite a galla day and I'm sure we almost won the war. I do wish tho dearest you could have seen our "tea fight".

That reminds me, I'm getting to be a regular old "tea hound" now. Several of us go over to the mess and make tea on a spirit lamp every afternoon and have become such beastly "tea hounds" that we get sore when anything interferes. What do you know about that? I'll promise to get rid of all my bad habits tho dearest before I come home.

Since my other letter sweetheart I have two more nights of flying behind me. Got to bed early last night (2 a.m.) so I'm up in time for dinner today. I was rotten last night, could fly alright but just lacked my usual easy touch and judgment. Wouldn't bother me if I didn't make the grade as a night flyer and got put on day work entirely for I have no love for this business of flying blind and just a little of it goes a long way with me. Just frazzles me out. I can do it alright however.

It certainly would have been hard luck sweetheart if I had been trained over there and sent to L. Charles finishing school. Wouldn't it? Why I could have flown home and landed in the park in 2 or 2 and a half hours.

By the way sweetheart we wear the silver U.S. wings now

(R.M.A. eagle) and the gold eagle was Italian. That is what their flyers wear. The Minister of War of Italy has authorized us to wear their gold eagle because we are Italian trained but John J. P. doesn't want us to wear it. Also that belt with the shoulder strap is called a "Sam Browne" belt and all officers on active service on this side of the water are required to wear it. It is quite a highly polished nifty affair.

Sweetheart you've made a bargain! If you really promise to look just as pretty and sweet as the last 14th of July I'll lick the whole German army to come home and I'll promise to come too, when this argument over here is settled. You'll have to go some dearest to be as wonderful as you were then but I'm sure my big baby can do it if she doesn't go and neglect herself for Pauline. That's one reason darling why I must insist that you always keep someone to assist you with Pauline. And I'll be miserable if you dont. So please dearest dont think of the small amount it takes to keep them, it's nothing for the amount of comfort I get out of it alone.

Just think honey its almost the 19th and when I left I thought sure I'd see you again before this. Well I'll surely see you again before the next 14th rolls around. So stiffen up your little upper lip (wish I could kiss it) and dont be so blue. Hear honey? It would help me so much if I could think of you as being happy and contented. If there is any change that could be made for your happiness sweetheart dont hesitate to tell me for you know that is my biggest desire.

Listen sweetheart I'm going to be good and 'fess up. Perhaps this night flying is making me superstitious. If it dont drive me batty it ought to do that. But about a month ago I carelessly sent my shirt to wash with your little medal pinned to the inside of the pocket and when the shirt came back it was gone. You dont know how bad that made me feel. I have the other but it wont stand wear precious, so cant you get me another just like that one I lost and send it to me?? Right away?? I have one of the silver name plates you wear around your wrist now and I want one just like that one I lost to fasten on the chain. Forgive me?

That's certainly news sweetheart about Marge Henry and Oswald Montaguet but I have heard somewhere before that he came to see her. Well Oswald used to be a straight forward dependable old boy even if he couldn't talk straight and will make her a good husband. I know he's getting a mighty fine girl but I dont envy anybody their girl since I got The Girl. You sweet precious thing. The old Censor will probably think I'm getting "mushy minded" but then he doesn't know you.

Sweetheart, do I send you enough money? I can send more precious and I want you to have plenty. Tell me dear?

I'd give anything to see that adorable little kid now. Just watch her coo and kick. Are you as lonesome sweetheart since you have her? Yes I got all the pictures, and you know sweetheart how precious they are to me. That was a cute sign you all had on the car in the parade.

I'm sending you two little pictures of myself and my two bunkies, just to show you how U. Sam's flying lieutenants really look off duty. These three "boys" (note ball headed one in middle) are merely taking their ease now. One of them seems to have a flea under his shirt. The big one is Spence Hart from Virginia who knows Johnny Pender and several old V.M.I. Cronies of mine. I just want you to see us as we ordinarily really are. E tardi! I must get ready to fly again tonight. Be two sweet babies and kiss each other a thousand times for Daddy. Dont you worry about me babykins. I'm alright and as safe, contented and well as can be. I'm looking out for my two babies interests. With a million long-kisses and hugs and all my love.

Your Devoted
Paulie.

O.K.
Paul M. Potts Jr.
1st Lt. A.S.Sig. R.C.

—

Silver Eagle identification bracelet for 1st Lieut. P. M. Potts, Jr., U.S. Air Service. Engraved on the back is Natchitoches, Louisiana, U.S.A.

1st Lieut. Potts' Silver Caproni pin presented to Caproni fliers. Caproni means Goat in Italian. At the time, the Caproni was the largest bomber in the war.

Pilots might have flown upside down without knowing it.

H'd'qs American Air Service
Rome Italy.
July 17th 1918

Dearest Babykinses:

Well I'm here. Where that is I have to keep a secret but I dont expect to be here long before I move on again. This is a very nice place and I'm enjoying life more than I have any where else in Italy. We have the nicest place to go swimming imaginable and we spend a couple of hours every day at it. Not doing much flying at present. Just eating good food and sleeping lots and swimming a little. What do you know about this? I have a valet. All Italian officers have them and since I'm with them I have to conform more or less to their habits. "My man" shines my shoes and leggings every day, wakes me up in the morning, sews buttons on my clothes etc. It seems funny to us for over home we take care of ourselves.

The last I wrote you Earl F. and I were trying to finish up our night flying back at the 8th A.I.C. (?) and weren't enjoying it very much. Well we finally got to our brevetto and on an awful dark morning about 3 a.m. We could fly very well at lower

JULY 17, 1918

altitudes but when we got up about 6000 ft. every thing was so black and the clouds obscured the horizon so that we simply slid rolled and lurched around on up to 10,000 ft. (Sometimes I think we must have turned upside down.) We couldn't tell a thing about our position except from the instruments and had to keep flashing the lights on them every 5 seconds. It felt real spooky to sit up there and think you were flying straight and level and then all of a sudden see one of the couple of stars that could be seen at times start moving around you in a circle and realize that you had gotten off balance and were cocked up in a tight spiral. When we touched the 10,000 level our time was up and we didn't lose any time cutting the motors and starting for the little thread of searchlight way below. Earl started driving us down but lost his sense of balance and had us going like a roller coaster. I took it then and Earl would watch the altimeter and call off our altitude as we went down, every hundred meters. I never worked so hard before as I did estimating our distance and getting us down into that light. It sure felt good too when it at last just caught us and we could see again. Now night flying holds no uncertainty for us. We've flown on the darkest night and got away with it so I have now built up my confidence in it. Funny how you work your confidence up that way.

I haven't had a letter from you kids in three weeks (no two weeks) and it seems like months. I rather think it will be quite a while before I get any more of your letters too, sweetheart, for I'll be on the go more or less and my address now is rather vague. I'll make out the best I can tho so don't you worry about that babykins. Just keep on writing. And I'll be perfectly alright and safe.

I was simply overjoyed to get away from where I was. Couldn't tell you while I was there what a miserable place it was. The contrast between it and my present surroundings is so great that just being here keeps me in good spirits. This is a beautiful country.

I wonder lots how you two kids are, what you're doing

and if you're cheerful. That's why you should write me cheerful encouraging letters as much as possible dearest, for you see my mail may be cut off any time, and you'd like me to have a cheerful letter to go on wouldn't you?? I'd give anything to see you, then I'm sure you wouldn't be blue again, and perhaps this old war wont last so much longer dear. You two kids take care of yourselves until I get back and then I'll do it for you. Be good now and dont worry a bit. Kiss each other a thousand times for Daddy. With a million kisses and all my love

Your Devoted
Paulie.

Use this address temporarily.
Paul M. Potts Jr.
1st Lt. A.S.Sig. R.C.
U.S. Air Service   A.E.F.
c/o American Aviation Headquarters
Rome, Italy.
(Hotel Royal)

Two pilots, one American and one Italian, and
two Italian machine gunners constituted a team.

American Exp. Forces in Italy
July 20th 1918

My darling Babykinses:
Your very sweet letter dated June 10th reached me at the
camp near Milan where I wrote you from last and it was so
sweet that it made me terribly homesick for you two kids. The
two pictures of my "kids" which you put in it
were the sweetest, cutest pictures you've sent me
yet. That girl of ours certainly has a disdainful
look. I'll bet she gives the boys a lot of trouble
some day. She's as cute as can be and I'm so
proud of her. But she couldn't be anything but wonderful with
such a little mother. It seems impossible, sweetheart, for me to
completely realize when I look at her picture that you and I are
responsible for her.

JULY 20,
1918

For the last few days and nights I've been traveling and
waiting for trains, the last more than the first. I arrived here
30 or 35 miles behind the lines yesterday. I am quartered in a
small village, and our machines and camp is possibly two miles
from us. When the major wants any of us to fly he sends a car.
There are seven of us all told and Curt Keen is one of them,
the others you dont know. We are detached from our air service

and attached to an Italian squadron, for how long I dont know but possibly a couple of months. Our squadron commander, a young Italian major of about thirty years is a splendid fellow and we are glad to be in his command. As for that matter all our brother Italian officers in our squadron are a fine bunch of men. You cant imagine how nice they are to us. This squadron, the 14th Squadriglia Caproni 500HP doesn't do any active work for a while yet, just getting things organized for business but we are going to do a lot of pratice (*sic*) flying with our teams to develop team work. An American pilot and an Italian pilot and two Italian machine gunners constitute a team. The Italians are experienced and are to show us the ropes. It's pretty good.

The major and six other Italian officers and ourselves have a mess here in town and we have very good food and service but possibly too much wine for Americans. We all have separate rooms in different parts of the town and very good ones too! Three of us have our rooms with the same family. My room is nicely furnished and comfortable and the signora keeps it spotlessly spick and span. If you could just see me dearest I know you'd want to use a rolling pin on my bean for being in such a nice war.

My meals cost me from 80 cents to $1.00 a day and my room and service about a quarter. So you see it's not bad. I'd like to send you another draft but I dont know when our quartermaster will come up in this neck of the woods to pay us so honey will have to wait until he does.

Our brother Italian officers are very friendly to us and we are very seldom together ourselves but go about usually with them so I have to parlare so much Italian that I get queer phrasing, and I suspect spelling, when I go back to English. So forgive me for anything queer in this letter. I cant speak Italian, I merely do the best I can to make myself understood by them. I hope to be able to speak it fluently in time.

With your letter dearest I also received one from Mother dated June 11th and one from Walter McCook. Tell mama I had begun to think she and Dad had allmost (*sic*) forgotten their soldier but I forgive her after that nice letter. Walter doesn't give me much dope about himself mostly asks about me, but I judge he is fixed well enough.

Curt Keen would tickle you to death sweetheart to see him ambling around. He "rubbers" at everything, be it a private garden or a military secret he butts right in. He and a little Italian lieut. are great chums. Keen calls him "mia picolina oca" (my little goose) and he calls Keen "alto" (high). They are very funny at meals.

I have some good pictures to send you darling that I left in Rome to be developed. Did I tell you that in Naples I picked up four little cameos and a couple of corral (*sic*) trinkets? They may not be any good but you get them from an old robber who makes them himself and sells them for almost nothing. So I sent them to you. One is for Mama. I was not allowed to send them mounted so when you get enough money you can have them mounted if you like.

I'll have to stop now or I'll be getting too homesick for my two bambinos. So sweetheart, "odesso la mia ragazzina," dont worry a bit about your Daddy for I'm alright. Sono sempre bene!!! Anche, sei bene? Be two sweet girls and love Dad lots, as he does you. With a million long kisses and hugs and all my love,

Your Devoted
Paulie.

Address –
1st Lt. Paul M. Potts Jr.
c/o Headquarters American Aviation
Hotel Royal, Rome
Am. Exp. F

c/o 14th Squadriglia Caproni
Don't use.

Mrs. Paul M. Potts Jr.
Natchitoches
Louisiana
U.S.A. (Stati Uniti)

No. I. I'm starting a system of cards since I don't get time to write so often(?) I know you wonder when it was I wrote so often. It is still a good war and I'm alright. Be good and don't worry

July 23rd 1918, Lovingly Paul.

ROMA - Fontana Trevi

14* Squad. Ca 5
Zona di Guerra
July 26 1918

My darling precious Babykinses:

Day before yesterday I received your sweet letter dated June 12th with the second pair of pictures of my two kids in it. Those two pictures are the first two you've sent me that realy (*sic*) look like you. The other two show baby up more but those last two look almost as good as our little mother really

JULY 26, 1918

does look. The one with you and baby sitting down hugging each other is a dream and almost makes me jealous! You cant imagine sweetheart what a joy those pictures are to your lonesome Daddy. They are almost like a kiss, each one. Listen precious you remember how I use to kid you about your "turned up" nose? You know I always did love the way that little nose turned up". So sometime soon doll up and take me a profile picture or so, hear? A mechanic down at Foggia who was an ornamental wood worker made me a lovely little picture frame out of the broken pieces of a smashed, walnut propeller blade and I keep it full of the pictures of my two kids on my dresser sempre. But I like a change every once in a while so I take out old pictures and put in new ones.

I'm glad our Mother has taken a house darling and it will

be just the thing for you and baby to divide your time with her and Mother Potts. I know you want to spend all your time with Mother Rollins while I'm gone dear, because you just need some one who is close to you, and I would say you could but you know sweetheart you and baby have grown into our Mother Potts affections and she'll miss you for she needs a daughter, so I'll just say divide up with our two mothers. How is that darling? I guess you've already gotten my letter fussing about those blue letters from you and have derived from it that I want you to stay with your Mother Rollins some. Since I got the letter saying "Mother is with us now" the blue letters have miraculously stopped coming and all your sweet letters have been as cheerful and sweet as any soldier husband could desire. So you see I can understand how you need our Mother Rollins when you haven't your Daddy.

So Mother and Dad didn't take to your offer of keeping house at one of the places, eh? Of course they know what a wonderful little housekeeper you are but they didn't want you to undertake so much sweetheart. You wait a while and then we'll keep house together at one of the places and run things to suit ourselves and just have a great old life. Wont we precious? Each day brings this old war 24 hours nearer the end and us a day nearer to each other, eh?

Listen sweetheart, I showed those last four pictures of my family to a couple of Italian officers in my squadriglia who are chummy with me and they said you and baby were beautiful and Mother Potts was nice and then they saw the one with Aunt Liz standing by you and it almost created a riot. They wanted to know if Aunt Liz was the babies other grandmother!!! They had never seen a negro!!! I didn't know the Italian word for "nurse" and we were in an awful fix. We finally cleared matters up by hunting up the Italian English dictionary and finding out what a nurse maid was. Then they understood fine and Aunt Liz's picture simply charmed them.

—

We are still in the process of organization sweetheart so I haven't taken that load of bombs over to Dutch yet but hope to soon. We have to get our machines ready and test them out to a fine point etc. They keep me pretty busy tho for we can't get through a meal in less than two hours and every day we have some sort of party in our honor. Yesterday it was a "drinking fest" with the mayor and town council, the day before we were invited up to a rich old citizen's home to drink wine with he and his family and the day before that it was a "drink fest" with the officers of another squadriglia and so on. We've all been on the verge of being drunk ever since we got here and don't know when we will have an opportunity to sober up. But seriously sweetheart, we are compelled, in the cause of sociability to consume an awful amount of wine and champagne for abstemious Americans. When I start flying I'll have to simply cut it out if it insults somebody for I cant drink and fly.

We really do have a right good time tho. They are all so nice to us. Don't you worry about the little wine I drink. We will soon have met everybody here and been intertained (*sic*) by them and then the formalities will be dispensed with. Our party today consisted of meeting the commanding colonel and he raised cain in general and gave everybody to understand that the squadron had to get down to business immediately. So here's hoping!

How about it sweetheart have you decided yet that you want to wear the polish off a rolling pin on me for living such an easy life on the front and making such a good war out of it?? I'll bet you do!

Now don't you spend one moment worrying about Daddy for it would be wasted and Daddy is looking after his two kids best interests. So be real good, take good care of yourself and kiss each other a million times for me. With a million kisses and hugs and all my love

Your Devoted
Paul

—

1st Lt. Paul M. Potts Jr.
c/o Headquarters American Aviation in Italy
Hotel Royal, Rome
American Exp. F.

Mrs. Paul M. Potts, Jr.
Natchitoches,
Louisiana, U.S.A.
Stati Uniti

Dearest. This is a picture of
the great curiosity, the one
armed clock. It always only
had one arm and never expected
to have any more. The people only
need to know the time approximately
you know. I was over here the other
day on bizz and took a look at it
my self. Be good. Everything is fine. Lovingly
July 28th 1918.   Paul.

BRESCIA – Torre detta la Pallata

American Exp. F.
14° Squad. Ca 5
Zona di Guerra
July 31st 1918.

Dearest Babykinses.

I'm longing for a letter from you but none comes. Sometime posibly some kind army postmaster will discover where I am and gather up the bunch of letters that I know are trying to find me and send them to me. This business of having such vague addresses down here is terrible. I just got a warning yesterday to under no circumstances have the number of my squadron put on the outside of an envelope. So dont put my squadron number on any of your letters until further word from me.

Earl and I had quite a bit of

2— excitement yesterday. Took off and our motors went bad just about 50 ft. up. The bad news part of it is that I was driving. We were right over the edge of our landing field pointing toward a little olive orchard. I tried to turn so as to hit the edge of our field but you cant turn one of these big old busses without any motors when you are only 50 ft. high, and I saw if I did turn we'd hit the ground turning which is real bad news when it happens, so I just ducked the nose straight ahead into the olive trees. The first tree we hit sounded pretty bad, worse than any of the subsequent ones we uprooted. We draped parts

<u>3</u>

of the poor old bus over every tree in that orchard. A part of a wing here, a wheel in that ditch another in this one, while Earl and I and the three motors and body sailed serenely on. I thought we simply never were going to hit something to stop us. We finally did stop though, with a little thump, still sitting serenely and unruffled in our seats. Then came the excitement, the explanation of what happened and why to the Italians. It was a whole lot harder for me to do that than to make up my mind to plow up that orchard. Of course I'm terribly sorry about the machine for there is so much to one of these 600 H.P's. but I'm very well satisfied that in an emergency I did the "safety first" thing.

= That is the first smash that has come any where near to being a real one that I have had and I wont do it again so dont worry.

Our quiet village life in the little town of G— still continues and would you believe it? our flight commander (an Italian captain) neither drinks wine nor smokes so now as he presides at the head of the mess none of us have to drink anything except water from now on. thats good news isn't it sweet heart?

In town here there is an old stone mill (water mill) that is the very image of the old mills you've seen pictured on the calendar. And it still grinds all the town's wheat! Curt and I went through it and watched them work and I know it has been there since the fall of Rome. I'm going to send you some pictures of it when I get them developed.

Listen dearest, I think I've written you four letters from here and some of them I put my squadrilia on the back as the Italians do, so now I dont know if they got through to you. I've also been sending you a lot of ~~picture~~ picture post cards and I dont know if they got through so tell me if they didn't.

Earl and I went to B— day before
yesterday. We got tired of the sponge
baths and decided to take a plunge
in a real tub. Well we went to the
hotel in B. and after laboring and perspiri
for ten minutes with the hotel clerk
trying in our best Italian to put
our idea across to him, that we didn't
want the hotel nor a room nor anything
to eat or drink but only wanted to
rent a bath room for an hour
we were just about to give up when
he was seized with a brilliant thought
and asked if we spoke English. The
"nut" spoke English almost as good as us!
We then found out that none of the
hotels in B— had running water and that

7/ over only chance for a bath was the public baths and that they were closed. So we didn't get a bath. Had to come back home and go to work harder than ever with our sponges. Darned if I see how these people keep so clean looking with their sponges!

Later. I was writing this out at camp this morning and as we were coming in in the car the chauffeur ran over a poor little tike about 5 yrs. old who started across the street ahead of us. The little fellow looked so awfully pitiful as he came rolling out from under the back end of the car that it nearly broke my heart. He miraculously came out with only a bad bruising and a very bad scalp wound. Get over it

8.

I've been getting more ~~chicken~~ chicken hearted sweetheart ever since I've been in this business. Every wreck I see affects me worse. I've got so that if I see I'm not positively needed I beat it out of sight when any thing happens. The last time I helped a rescue party git the men out of a wreck I was sick for three days afterwards. But the funny part is I dont mind it for myself, only for others. You'll be thinking this is a bad news letter if I dont wind up before I think of some more bad news so be good, both of you and take care of your sweet selves for Daddy. And dont worry about him. Kiss each other a million times for me and love me lots. With a million kisses and hugs and all my love.   Your Devoted Paulie.

Address— 1st Lieut. Paul M. Potts Jr.
Army Air Service Headquarters
Rome, Italy.
American Exp. Fr.
% Capt. La Guardia

❦ THE OLIVE ORCHARD ❦

American Exp. F.
14th Squad. Ca
Zona di Guerra
July 31st 1918

Dearest Babykinses,

I'm longing for a letter from you but none comes. Sometime possibly some kind army postmaster will discover where I am and gather up the bunch of letters that I know are trying to find me and send them to me. This business of having such vague addresses down here is terrible. I just got a warning yesterday to under no circumstances have the number of my squadron put on the outside of an envelope. So dont put my squadron number on any of your letters until further word from me.

Earl and I had quite a bit of excitement yesterday. Took off and our motors went bad just about 50 ft. up. The bad news part of it is that I was driving. We were right over the egde (*sic*) of our landing field pointing toward a little olive orchard. I tried to turn so as to hit the edge of our field but you can't turn one of these big old busses without any motors when you are only 50 ft. high and I saw if I did turn we'd hit the ground turning which is real bad news when it happens, so I just ducked the nose straight ahead into the olive trees. The first tree we hit sounded pretty bad, worse than any of the subsequent ones we

JULY 31,
1918

uprooted. We draped parts of the poor old bus over every tree in that orchard. A part of a wing here, a wheel in that ditch, another in this one, while Earl and I and the three motors and body sailed serenely on. I thought we simply never were going to hit something to stop us. We finally did stop though, with a little thump, still; sitting serenely and unruffled in our seats. Then came the excitement, the explanation of what happened and why to the Italians. It was a whole lot harder for me to do that then to make up my mind to plow up that orchard. Of course I'm terribly sorry about the machine for there is so much to one of these 600 H. P.'s. but I'm very well satisfied that in an emergency I did the "safety first" thing. That is the first smash that has come any where near to being a real one that I have had and I wont do it again so dont worry.

Our quiet village life in the little town of G— still continues and would you believe it? Our flight commander (an Italian captain) neither drinks wine nor smokes so now as he presides at the head of the mess none of us have to drink anything except water from now on. That's good news isn't it sweet heart?

In town here there is an old stone mill (water mill) that is the very image of the old mills you've seen pictured on the calendars. And it still grinds all the town's wheat! Curt and I went through it and watched them work and I know it has been there since the fall of Rome. I'm going to send you some pictures of it when I get them developed.

Listen dearest, I think I've written you four letters from here and some of them I put my squadriglia on the back as the Italians do, so now I dont know if they got through to you. I've also been sending you a lot of picture post cards and I dont know if they got through so tell me if they didn't.

Earl and I went to B- day before yesterday. We got tired of the sponge baths and decided to take a plunge in a real tub. Well we went to the hotel in B. and after laboring and perspiring for ten minutes with the hotel clerk trying in our best Italian to put our idea across to him, that we didn't want the hotel nor a room nor anything to eat or drink but only wanted to rent a bath room for an hour we were just about to give up when he was seized with a brilliant thought and asked if we spoke English. The "nut" spoke English almost as good as us! We then found out that none of the hotels in B- had running water and that our only chance for a bath was the public baths and that they were closed. So we didn't get a bath. Had to come back home and go to work harder than ever with our sponges. Darned if I see how these people keep so clean looking with their sponges!

Later. I was writing this out at camp this morning and as we were coming in the car the chauffeur ran over a poor little tike about 5 yrs. old who started across the street ahead of us. The little fellow looked so awfully pitiful as he came rolling out from under the back end of the car that it nearly broke my heart. He miraculously came out with only a bad bruising and a very bad scalp wound. Get over it.

I've been getting more chicken hearted sweetheart ever since I've been in this business. Every wreck I see affects me worse. I've got so that if I see I'm not positively needed I beat it out of sight when any thing happens. The last time I helped a rescue party get the men out of a wreck I was sick for three days afterwards. But the funny part is I dont mind it for myself, only for others. You'll be thinking this is a bad news letter if I don't wind up before I think of some more bad news so be good, both of you and take care of your sweet selves for Daddy. And dont worry about him. Kiss each other a million times for me and love me lots. With a million kisses and hugs and all my love.

Your Devoted Paulie.

1st Lieut. Paul M. Potts Jr.
Army Air Service Headquarters
Rome, Italy
American Exp. F. c/o Capt. La Guardia

———

14* Squadriglia Caproni
Zona di Guerra
Aug 3rd 1918

My precious Babykinses:-

Got your two letters dated June 20th and 23rd yesterday. I know there is a bunch of them in between these last two and the last ones I had received before so guess they will come straggling in.

Now see precious, you went and let the darned old newspaper get you to believing I was on the front a month before I'm even thinking of it and now you've been wasting a whole months

AUGUST 3, 1918

worry for that little brown head. And you forget dearest that I live way back out of all the excitement all the time except when I actually take a load of bombs over and I do that at night so they cant see me to shoot at me and the worst I have to fear is a forced landing and being captured and that's practically out of the question. Why my job will be such a "sinch" (*sic*) that I'm almost ashamed to call myself in the war. Also dearest I'm afraid it will be nothing short of two months before I get to "go over" and possibly longer so what have you to worry about now?? Don't do it!!

Yes sweetheart I'll promise you all over again to take just the best possible care of myself and come back safe to you.

You needn't bother that brown head one instant about me ever forgetting a single thing I promised you dearest for I'll promise you all over again that I wont. I dont want to forget any of them. I want to get back to my two kids again too bad for that.

Sweetheart you know there are no furloughs given back to America. We are here for the duration of the war. We are allowed 7 days out of every four months, "leave", but we have to spend it in the country we are in and if I dont take 7 days these four months then I cant wait and take 14 days in the next four months. Only 7. Cant save it up that way you see. There is not even any way to ask for a furlough.

Listen precious, talk it over with Dad and see what he thinks about taking that matter up with Dave B. and Mr. Aswell. The three of them might be able to fix it up in some special way. 'Specially Mr. Aswell. About November would be the best time to see about it. I really don't think we'd have a bit of luck tho' before next summer a year, and it's just barely possible they might be successful then. It wont do me a bit of harm for them to try it as much and as often as they will sweetheart and I certainly think we both need it and deserve it and I have thought of it as much as you dearest and want it just as bad. I dont think it's possible tho dearest but you never can tell.

Time keeps lengthening out dearest and I can say now it will be at least two months from now before I'll do any of the active work over the lines. I'm flying every day, enough to keep my hand in and I'll be some pilot (*sic*) in another month, handling bad motors. Getting lots of practice with them. Sometimes I fly with one of my brother Italian officers in our squadron and sometimes with one of the other fellows in our bunch, but most of the time with Earl Forsythe. I like to fly with him better than any one else for we both have confidence in each other and work together with the machine just as if we could read each other's mind. It takes two pilots to run this 600 it's such a tremendous machine. It's a good machine too. I like it.

I notice sweetheart in those last pictures of my two kids, Pauline is beginning to look as if she had a little mind of her own. How I wish I could see you both. Sweetheart I think in one of those last two pictures she looks just like you in that baby picture you gave me a long time ago. She does!

Kiss each other a thousand times for Daddy and be two real good girls. Now dont you worry for I'm perfectly alright sweetheart and will take the very best care of myself. With a million kisses and hugs and all my love

Your Devoted
Paul

O.K.
Paul M. Potts Jr.
1st Lt. A.S.Sig.R.C.

14* Squadriglia Ca 5
Zona de Guerra
American Exp. F. Aug. 10th

My precious Babykinses:-
How do you like the heading of my letter?? Yesterday I got your two sweet letters dated July 5th and July 10th. The one of the 5th had those two sweet pictures of Pauline in it. You just refuse to send me any more pictures of my "big kiddie" dont you?? Dont know what I'm going to do about it if you dont get busy and take me some good looking pictures of yourself also. I like my pictures of Pauline but you know I haven't entirely ceased to like to look at pictures of you also.

Day before yesterday Curt Keen and I were down at Milan on business for the day. I sent you a postcard picture of the very wonderful cathedral there. Didn't have time to go through it but would have liked to as it is noted throughout Italy. Had dinner at a German restaurant and drank some real German beer there (which made me sick, so I didn't want any supper). Had quite a nice visit with the Y.M.C.A. people there.

AUGUST 10, 1918

Now we are anxiously awaiting our quartermaster for last months pay. Looks as if we might not be paid for the next two months. It wont run for over another month tho without pay. Are you fixed well enough to make your visits this summer, that is cash enough on hand? You never tell me a blooming thing about how you are fixed financially sweetheart and so I never know whether what I send is just too little for you to bother about or whether it covers your needs. Please sweetheart keep me informed on how you are fixed so I wont worry if I dont need to and can send more if you need it for I could easily send more dearest on "pay days" without missing it a bit and the most pleasure I have is that of providing for my two kiddies. By the way darling in June I sent you a draft for $50 about the 18th and either a couple of weeks before or a couple later I sent you a money order for $50 together with one for Billie. Were all received?? When I'm paid again I'll send another.

Our Mother Rollins said you all would spend the time between the summer school and opening of her school just visiting around. I hope you did sweetheart for I'm getting worried about your sticking so close at home. Of course I know dearest that it's not your fault that you stick so close but (keep this secret) you just never did learn that Mother Potts just simply has to be "managed", like a child, did you? And that Dad has to be coaxed with good humor? And that I've known Mother Potts about 23 years now and as far back as I can remember she has always "fussed" the live long day through and that it doesn't mean a thing, she just has a nervous easily upset temperament. You just wont stand up for your rights dearest, just let any body "bulldoze" you and worry you and make you do things you dont want to. And I cant do a thing in the world for you dearest, not a thing, not until I get home. With every letter dear, from you, I realize that you are just as miserable as it is possible for a human to be and still live and that you've entirely given up hope of ever seeing me again. I lie awake some nights, wondering if there is anything on earth I could do to please you and make you forget for just a day how miserable you are. I wonder if it's my fault? Sometimes I think maybe it is and that I should have left you single, that you would be a thousand times happier that way, you could certainly not be any more miserable. Don't you know I'd come home if I could? Dont you know that the army is the same thing as prison as far as going where you want is concerned? I cant say to the authorities "here, my wife wants me to quit and come home so you'll get someone in my place". Listen dearest, as long as the war lasts, I'm compelled to stay over here. If you were dying I couldn't come to you, so for heavens sake honey make up your mind that you have to wait. Over here we are fighting the Germans and we dont find war entirely a bunch of roses, but I haven't complained much about it have I sweetheart? Haven't my letters up to date been cheerful? If we fight the war out over here and keep a cheerful atmosphere about us as we do it (and sometimes it's pretty hard to be cheerful) and we treat most everything as a joke and I know all my companions write cheerful letters home and get the same in reply and I've tried to do the same up to now. But this letter is the end of my attempts at cheerfulness with you honey for I see it's absolutely no use us trying to be cheerful with each other any more. It does seem to me tho darling that if we cheerfully put up with the hardships and risk our necks doing the fighting for you folks at home that you all could at least be as cheerful as we are about it. I'll be honest with you sweetheart, I'm getting pretty desperate over your letters. I love for you to confide your troubles to me dearest but have you stopped to think that you haven't confided a trouble to me for at least a month and that your letters have no troubles, you insist that you are all right and well cared for but you pour out several pages of just pure complaining against me, for being away from you and not coming home when you want me, for being over here in the war, for flying, for everything. Darling do you think I'm to blame for the whole blooming war? I didn't start the darn thing and I'm doing all they will let me to stop it. And I'm just not cut out to be a slacker and try to stay home and I'm not cut out to be a home guardsman or work in the quartermaster corps. Gee! But aren't you sorry I didn't stay home and claim exemption from the draft? You'd like me lots better wouldn't

—

you if I had faked epileptic fits or something to get to stay home with you instead of volunteering for the air service. Up until and a short while after little Pauline's advent you were an awful brave little girl and gave me lots of encouragement, but in the last few months you have just allowed yourself to go under until now I'm so discouraged over you that I almost wish a number of things, that you didn't have Pauline, that we hadn't been so hasty – I know you'd be happier any way but the way you are. And you've convinced me dearest that I alone am to blame for all your unhappiness and I'm sorry but there's nothing, absolutely nothing, I can do about it. You have to work the situation out for your little self.

Now enough of this, sweetheart, I hate to spoil a nice day for the Censor by making him read it. I know my poor little girl is having a hard life and it's wonderful of you to go on loving me through it all when I'm to blame for it. If it hadn't been for me you'd be a happy little imp dancing around the parties with the infants too young for the draft.

You didn't get my letter asking you not to try to take care of the "kiddie" yourself did you? It seems to me dearest that I asked you as an especial favor to me to keep a nurse for Pauline and to not wash her clothes even if you do "like" to. Now your letter says, "I've done away with Pauline's nurse and spent the morning washing her clothes." Why??? Can't you afford the two or three dollars a week? If you cant sweetheart I can over here so just borrow the money from Dad or Mother Rollins and get them to send the bill to me. So – once more I ask you dearest as an especial favor to me (will you do it?) hire a nurse to do all the heavy work of looking after Pauline and keep her till I come home. And dont be washing baby clothes, for I'll admit it's purely selfishness in me, I dont fancy having a wife with a pair of washwoman's hands. Now will you be good?

A while ago just after I started writing this the mail orderly brought me your letter dated June 25th. Can you guess what point it was in this letter that I stopped to read it?

I hope dearest that you'll stay on with Mother Rollins for I feel like you will be a little better off staying with her while I'm away. Let me know when you settle down at Kelly and I'll send your letters there as they will possibly reach you sooner. I would have cabled you from up here but there is no cable office I can get to as there was in Foggia. Be good and take good care of my big and little kiddie. With a million kisses and hugs and all my love

Your Devoted
Paul.

Paul M. Potts Jr.
1st Lieut A.S.Sig. R. C.

Though actual speed was not spelled out in these letters, the average speed in 1914 was recorded at 60 miles per hour.

14* Squadriglia Ca
Zona di Guerra
Am. Exp. F.
Aug. 12th 1918.

My dearest Babykinses:-

Just got your letter of June 17th this morning so you see how the mail man is doing me as I already have your other letters up to July 11th.

This letter of the 17th is really very cheerful so I'm just pretending dear that it is the last letter instead of the first and that you're in a cheerful frame of mind instead of the dugeons (*sic*). So you take Pauline visiting eh? Bet you wish you had me there to leave her with while you call. I'd have liked to have seen her trying to ruin Mrs. Phelps floor.

Listen dearest I'm sure, handling Pauline so much can't be good for that weak little back of yours, and I wish so much honey you'd take care of yourself and not make an invalid out of yourself before I come back. So wont you try to get a nurse for Pauline and keep her? It would make me feel that you are taking much better care of yourself if you will. I'm afraid you'll make a regular invalid out of yourself before I come back and that would be pretty bad for us dearest.

No I certainly wont bump you around in a car "when I come home" sweetheart. Flying hasn't made me a speed maniac or any thing like that. It has had just the reverse influence on me and made me more cautious. Why I'm even afraid to ride a bicycle fast now. And the street cars in Milan just made my heart stick to the roof of my mouth. Up in the air you crave speed. Just itch for it for it's speed that holds you up there and there is no feeling so helpless as to lose speed in the air. But not on the ground. "Uh Uh not me!" The minute my foot touches the ground all desire for speed ceases entirely. I just want to walk around very slowly. So you needn't be afraid that I wont be able to drive us around to suit you. You'll probably scare me to death making me drive fast enough to suit you.

Well dearest, what did you do about V. (*sic*) L.R. and the job. It's amusing that he'd make such a rash promise so hastily but then maybe he thinks I wont get back. There is where he gets fooled tho' dearest for it's been decreed that nothing is going to happen to me and I'm coming back. I have the most wonderful luck of any body you ever saw. What I do when I get back tho' sweetheart depends entirely on what you want me to.

Got a nice letter from Bob and he said Mother was looking awful badly when he was home. He was carried away with Pauline. If Mother goes out to Lillian's, Sis is going to just worry her to death for you have no idea what a "slave driver" Sis is. After Sis visits home Mother used to be completely exhausted. I'm awful afraid they are going to ruin her health. You and Mother are just alike in that respect. Neither of you will declare your rights with those dear to you and just let them impose on you. If I ever get home tho' there's going to be an end of this business of any body imposing on you. Not even Pauline! Only me.

Now you've left me without knowing what you are going

to do with yourself for the next month or so. One letter says you will visit around with Mother Rollins and another says you are glad you dont have to and can just go out to the woods of Kelly and rest for a few months. Now which did you do? I'm glad you are going to do one or the other dearest. Just so you get away from Natchitoches and stay where Mother Rollins can look after you awhile and cheer you up. You need the change.

Sweetheart I'm absolutely certain you haven't gotten half the letters I've been writing you. It has been very seldom that I've gone 10 days without writing you and I've always mentioned it in the one or two cases where I have. I've been writing you about three times a week from here and sending you a card on days when I didn't write. Have you been getting them? I wrote you a rather discouraged, fussy letter day before yesterday darling cause your gloomy letters were just worrying me to death sweetheart. Please cheer up for Daddy, hear? Be a good little wife now and tell Pauline to be good too and kiss each other a thousand times for me. With a million long long kisses and hugs and all my love

Your Devoted
Paulie

O.K.
Paul M. Potts Jr.
1st Lieut. A.S.Sig. R.C.

<hr>

§ TWO MOTORS GONE ç

<hr>

Zona di Guerra, Italia
3 Septembre 1918

My dearest Babykinses:-

I have just gotten settled again after – to use the army phrase – "a change of station". You know I wrote you from Ghedi last week that we were going to fly over to a different camp. Wal we've done done hit.

Yesterday the postman brought me an awful nice bunch of letters, there was a recent one from Walter up on the north coast of England in answer to my letter to him, one from Cousin Mary, a nice one too, one from our paymaster with a check for my July pay in it and last and best three from my babykinses dated July 14th, 16th and 19th with more sweet pictures in them. Mary was real nice and told me lots about Shirley and Pauline. If I didn't know before that the young Pauline was the most remarkable person in seven states I know it now sweetheart after hearing Mary rave about her. Yes, I truly love her almost as much as I do you and I'm just as proud of both of you as I can be and still condescend to associate with my fellow man.

SEPTEMBER 3, 1918

A secret, sometime ago Bob wrote me that Mama needed a rest something terrible and that I ought to write her and tell her to go to see him and Margaret in August so they would give her a rest. I did so, but I knew it was not for a rest that

198

he wanted Mama. I dont blame him for wanting her down there but he should come out and say what for. Another secret, he wrote me that Papa had "thrown" away $7000.00 recently in the last half year on Shirley, Pauline, the car and family". I immediately wrote him back that he was mistaken badly about Papa throwing away his money on my two kids for all they got from Dad was board and room, little enough, and that my two kids lived on their own Daddy's money. Don't breathe a word of this sweetheart to anybody. I'm just telling you for your own edification. Capito? But you can just put this in your little brown head and keep it there. No body, not a single one of Mother's daughters has been half, even a fourth as considerate of Mama as you have. So you quit worrying about how Mama talks about the independence of Lillian and Margaret. To them she'll talk more of the independence and consideration of you. I know her. So don't you worry about that.

You know I told you I was going to fly my machine down to our new camp. Well there was nothing to that, all the other machines made the trip without trouble except mine and for a whole day I had a very unique time for I had a forced landing. We were breezing along about 12000 ft up, myself and an Italian sergeant, driving alternately, with an Italian lieutenant observer up in the front seat when the rear motor broke it's crank shaft and almost tore itself loose with the vibration before we stopped it. We didn't think much of that, being only a half hour distant from out destination and thought we could make it if the other two motors kept working. We kept losing altitude then until we were only about 3000 ft. up when one of the side motors got too hot and quit on us. You can't go far with only one motor working so then we got pretty darned busy looking for a soft spot to set the old bus down in. It takes an extra lot of ground room and extra smooth ground to land these machines in at all safely, they are so big and turn over and "sqush" you under the motors so easily so you can imagine how busy that sergeant and myself were looking for the best field in reach. The poor observer (I wouldn't be an observer for anything) was just throwing one fit after another. From even 3000 ft. the ground looks pretty much the same all over and you can't tell what's smooth and what's rough but in about 2 seconds we picked us the best looking field in reach and were diving down to it. Out of the corner of my eye the sergeant didn't look "fussed" at all so I decided since he had been flying a year longer than I had I'd leave it up to him to make the landing. The field was a cow pasture and I know we scared about five years growth out of a bunch of calves that were in it. The sergeant made a beautiful tail low landing so smooth that in spite of the fact that when we got right down on it we saw the pasture had little ditches running all over it we only broke one brace wire. Then the fun, or I should say the trouble, began. In ten minutes after we landed there were a thousand people packed around that machine and in half an hour there were at least five thousand. All the countryside for ten miles around had seen us go down and rushed to the spot to have a "look, see". It was the first aeroplane they had ever seen there and I was the first American they had even heard of. I was amused at a veterinary sergeon (*sic*) who had run his horse to the spot from three miles away in hope as he frankly stated that his services were needed.

We finally got a detail of soldiers from a nearby artillery camp posted over the machine as guards to keep the populace from carrying it away piece meal for souvenirs and a carriage from the artillery camp to take us to a village where we could phone the news back to camp. At the village we had to wait until late in the evening to get transportation on to our destination and we were just like animals in a menagerie. The crowd followed us about everywhere, the telephone girl tried to flirt with us and every time we stopped the crowd packed around us so close we didn't have breathing space.

—

We finally found a café with a private back room where we fastened ourselves in to get relief from the open mouthed staring populace. When we finally arrived at our destination the rest of the fellows who had all made the trip without trouble were out looking for us since they had every report imaginable, from the one which said we were all three killed and the machine a total wreck on up to the one which said we had turned around and gone back to our starting point.

Now I'm under the command of a famous Colonel (Italian). He is the most famous Caproni bombing pilot on this front and honest if he gets even one more medal I'll be darned if I see where he'll wear it for when he "dolls up" his medals and decorations completely cover his manly breast. There are only about a dozen of us (officers) at the camp here now and we all room in the same barracks which has our dining room in one end of it. Wonderful food but no water! Can you imagine drinking light wine altogether instead of water? I haven't had a drink of water for three days now except for one glass of mineral water with each meal. The doctor won't let us drink the water at all until he gets a system installed for purifying our drinking water, which he promises to do soon. It better be soon!

The Colonel has a pair of pet monkeys and it's absolutely the funniest thing I ever saw to see him with them. They idolize him, crawl up on his shoulder and kiss his cheeks, pet him on the face like he does them, pull his mustache and rummage through his hair looking for fleas. They also unbutton the flaps on his pockets and go through them taking every thing out. They keep the whole bunch of us in a good humor with their pranks.

The Colonel said Curt Keen and I were to go after my machine as soon as a new motor had been put in it, when we were at dinner today. I have the nicest room you ever saw sweetheart all to myself, but more of that later. Be two real good girls and dont worry about Daddy for I'm alright and contented and safe. Kiss each other a thousand times for me, and hurry up those big pictures. With all my love and a million long kisses and hugs.

Your Devoted,
Paulie

O.K.
Paul M. Potts Jr.
1st Lieut A.S.Sig.R.C.

ര MY NEW CAMP ര

Zona di Guerra, Italia
Sept. 4th 1918.

Dear Mother Rollins:-

I have your letter of July 8th and I feel like I have you to thank for getting my two kids into a better frame of mind. Just before you joined Shirley in Natchitoches she was feeling awful discouraged but since you've been with her, her letters have been all that any soldier could ask for. I'm surely glad you are fixed now so she can stay with you as much as she wants. She's an awful brave little girl but when she gets away from her mother and her Paul too she gets pretty low spirited.

I've been telling her if she dont get a nurse and washwoman for Pauline and keep them she'll be looking all worn out when I come home and I wont stay, so she's got some large pictures of herself and Pauline on the way to show me how good looking my two kids are. It simply worries me to death to think of her taking care of Pauline alone and I've fussed at her until I cant say anything more trying to get her to keep help. But she just wont and ignores it and goes right ahead telling me how much she has to do looking after Pauline. It runs me wild. She did say that she'd have a girl to help her some at your house. Wont you try to make her keep help when she is with you?

Shirley told Mary Haynes she could write me some news

SEPTEMBER 4,
1918

203

so Mary wrote me a long letter telling me all the gossip about almost every body I've known in the last few years, but what tickled me was she claimed Pauline bore a resemblance to her. Everybody who writes me claims that Pauline looks like them.

A few days ago I moved from my old camp to a new camp on a different part of the front and Shirley can tell you what a time I had getting here. I've practically quit mentioning flying where Shirley can get a hold of it for I think if I'll keep quiet about my flying and experiences she'll forget what I'm doing to some extent and stay in better spirits.

At my new camp I'm fixed awful comfortably. Nice room, excellent food and I'm under the command at present of an Italian Colonel whom I like very much. He has a pair of pet monkeys and I spend hours watching them and laughing at them for they are absolutely the funniest clowns I ever saw. The Colonel also has a big Newfoundland dog and the monkeys take him down every day and pick the fleas off him. They love the Colonel almost humanly, climb up on his shoulder and pet and caress his cheeks and ruffle his hair. The aviation service is the greatest branch of the army for pets, of all I think. I'm well, safe, and as contented as can be. Keep my girl cheerful.

Lovingly
Paul.

Address-
1st. Lieut. Paul M. Potts Jr.
c/o Commando d'Aeronauticaa disposizione
Zona di Guerra, Italia.
American Exp. Forces

O.K.
Paul M. Potts Jr.
1st Lieut. A.S.Sig. R.C.

❧ THE COLONEL'S PET, LULU ❧

Zona di Guerra,
Italia
5 Settembre 1918

My dearest Babykinses:-

Just a short note this morn for the purpose of enclosing this $50.00 draft to you. When you get it dearest mention in at least two letters that you have it and refer to it as dated Sept 3rd.

I haven't heard from you in regard to the two money orders I sent to you and Billie for $50 and $25 and I feel like it is about time I was getting a letter saying you have received them. I have your cable and letter telling me you have the draft of about June 18th.

The order to pay us flying pay has at last come through and from now on I'll be getting around $220.00 per so I can well afford to send you plenty now. And dont worry or imagine for one minute that I'll be stinting myself for I'll promise for your own ease of mind I'll keep plenty with me for all my needs. I dont like to send large amounts by these drafts, so will just save it up until I get to see a quartermaster, which will be in the next month or so and then allot you several months salary together which will be paid from Washington. Meantime dear I'll send you these $50.00 drafts about once a month for your running expenses. So dear, you and our daughter will be provided

SEPTEMBER 5, 1918

for much better before long and can start yourselves a real bank account.

One of those darned monkeys of the colonel's, (he turns one loose and keeps the other chained) has pushed my door open and is sitting there making faces at me. His name is Lulu and he is just a little afraid of me. Dont know how to figure out my character I suppose for sometimes I cajole him and give him chocolate and sometimes I yell at him and scare him half out of his skin. This morning he slipped in my room and grabbed up a new flashlight bulb off my table and beat it through the window with it. I was still in bed and I let out a terrific yell which scared him so he fell off the window sill in his haste to get out. My man came rushing in thinking I'd thrown a fit or had an attack of the "D.T's." and he had to chase Lulu for about an hour all over the camp before he got the bulb away from the old thief. He went in Curt Keen's room yesterday and made off with his tooth brush and when next seen was up on the roof having a great time tickling himself with the stiff bristles. Last night he stopped supper proceedings three times while the Colonel had to go get him out of trouble in different parts of the camp. The last time the Colonel got sore and spanked him and made him sit in the corner of the mess hall until we finished, saying he was going to see whether he or Lulu was the commander of this camp.

The Colonel is a most likeable commander, awfully strict on duty, but around barracks with his pets and us he's like a pranking boy. We have lots of leisure as this is a quiet season for us. All we have in the line of duty is to make a lazy bunch of mechanics and cleaners polish up our machines daily. So dont worry about my safety sweetheart. I hope this letter with this draft dont get lost. Be good, both of you, and kiss each other many times for Daddy. With a million long kisses and hugs and all my love

Your Devoted
Paul.

O.K.
Paul M. Potts Jr.
1st Lieut. A.S.Sig. R.C.

Lt. Paul Potts is second from left.

Letter dated September 4, 1918, transcribed in Notes, p. 256.

Ragnelli caught treating
to chocolate. In back ground
is Minardis the sergeant who
flew with me down to the new
camp and landed our bus in
the cow pasture.

Pica and Vertus,
the mascot.

More Pica and Vertus
with the action on the Vertus.

That's me! Keen caught
me coming from this little
church one Sunday morn
and took my picture in the act.
"The camera's eye dont lie."

Some of the powers that were in my former squadron.

This is the way the ground looks from 6000 ft. Curt Keen was driving while I took this picture. The film was splotched some.

The famous headless statue of Rome.

A glimpse of the famous old Tiber River where it flows through Rome.

Entrance to the king's palace in Rome.

Fragmentary glimpses of "my old bus" which I'm hoping the censor will pass but am afraid he won't.

With a million kisses to you both and all my love, be good,

Your devoted

That's me!

𐆛 FIRE OFFICER 𐆜

Zona di Guerra, Italia
American Exp. F.
16 Settembre 1918

My darling Babykinses-

I now have your sweet letters of July 23rd and 25th and August 6th, 9th and 10th. That is pretty nice dearest as it brings your letters up to when the most recent is only a month old instead of a month and a half or two months as they have been coming ever since I left Foggia.

You two kids do get the queerest notions sometimes – your letter of Aug. 10 completely puzzled me for awhile until I got it figured out. You remember you were answering my letter of July 17th and said you hoped I was having a nice time in Rome. Well dearest that letter was written up near Milan and I had only stopped in Rome for six hours on the way up, three days before. Do you wonder it befuddled me and made me afraid I had had too much wine with some of my meals? So I figured it out that my letters were sent back to Rome and postmarked there and too I had given you my address in care of Rome, but that was merely so my letters would be sent direct to Rome and readdressed to my squadron from there. See? It sure did puzzle me for awhile tho.

Yes dearest, I really am fixed up better and more comfortably up here on the front now than I have been before.

SEPTEMBER 16,
1918

Wonderful food, I'm getting as fat as a pig, a delightful room all to myself positively luxuriously furnished, a "man" to bring me coffee in bed in the mornings, keep my clothes in shape and my room, plenty of American smokes from the Y.M.C.A. and to top it off with, we have an auto with a chauffeur all complete to drive us to town whenever we want to go. Now- if that's not a life of luxury for a fellow on the front I'll just eat my hat. Anybody who could treat us nicer or fix us up more comfortably than the Italian army has would have to go some. I'm for Italy strong now.

Of course, sweetheart, don't think we accept and take advantage of this hospitality without trying to be deserving of it. No, we do our "darnedest", fly whenever, whatever and wherever they'll let us and hold ourselves always ready for anything. You know as I told you before we are detached from the American army and are attached to the Italian air service as officers in their squadriglia. It's an interesting life.

Right at present Curt and I are undergoing a forced rest from flying of a few weeks because our machines are in the hospital awaiting "operations" so the Colonel (Italian) called us over to his office the other morning and through the interpreter told us that we were put under his command to take up the duties of Italian flying officers and that when we were not flying he'd have to use us for Italian non flying officers, so I would be "fire officer", he gave me a title a yard long which meant "fire officer" when you boil it down to pocket size, and would take a company of Italian soldiers and "test out the fire apparatus" of the camp. He went on to tell us that if any of the men we were given, shirked work or refused to take our orders we were to sentence them to a period in the guard house. The interpreter turned to us and said, "The colonel say if he no do to suit you, you can put him in prison." We had understood what the Colonel had said in Italian and naturally didn't think much of what the interpreter had said. Curt was given a bunch of gardeners and ditch diggers and told to drain and beautify the camp If the Colonel had led a fine, fat, white elephant into the office and said, "Take him and keep him" we'd have looked and felt just about the same. Well – I staggered out and found my company of would be fire fighters and led them over to the garage where the "fire apparatus" was, consisting of half dozen or so motor pumps, the like of which I had never seen before. I knew they were to be run with gasoline 'cause they had gasoline engines on them and after about half an hour while "my company" stood around and eyed first me and then the pumps, I figured out which end the water went in and which end it came out. But what worried me was where we were to find any water in this dry camp. I didn't know what to do so I started in to "ball out" the interpreter for not being able to talk any English. He could understand just enough to know he was getting "balled out" so he started to haranguing the men. The effect was marvelous – they rushed at the pumps, rolled them out of the garage and started off down the road with them "lickety split" with me chasing along behind wondering what the deuce would happen next. A canal borders our camp on one side and they lined those pumps up in a nice symmetrical row on the bank of it and connected them up ready to run in about two minutes. Then everything stopped and they started eyeing first me and the pumps again. I in turn examined the pumps very absorbedly as if I could find out from them what I was supposed to do. Finally it came to me, they were waiting for me to say the word for them to start pumping. I hastily let 'em know I was ready and they started the first one. Like an "ignorant nut" I was standing right in front of the nozzle and when the motor started a stream of water that looked as big as a barrel shot over my head just missing me by half an inch, I saved myself from being drowned by an acrobatic feat and strategically entrenched myself on the other side of the canal before I gave the word to start the others. The soldiers all stood around and blinked as solemn as a bunch of owls and I glared my fiercest at them but I know they would have all howled with laughter if they hadn't been afraid to. After we got them all going good the Colonel came out and squirted water all over everything and everybody, as tickled as a kid with a new toy. Since then one of the Italian lieutenants who is quite an artist has drawn this picture of me and started to put under it "Commander of the fire brigade" but he didn't know how to spell it. Keen says that's the way I'll look after two more years of the war. I've enclosed the picture. Now almost every day some new job turns up that I know about as much of as I did of those pumps and we get in very funny situations.

There you are babykinses, worrying about me and my safety all the time, when absolutely all there's any use worrying is just a little bit about once a month. All the other time I'm leading just as safe an existence as I would be at home. Dearest the war is not all blood and thunder by a long way. So quit worrying about me so much.

One thing tho' honey, if worrying will keep you from getting too fat then do just enough to keep the surplus fat off. Dont know why but I've suddenly become smitten with a terrible fear that you are going to get fat, too fat, a double chin and all that. Dont you do it. Stay just like you were last July a year ago –

Not a bit fatter! Hear??? I won't come home if you dont!!??

Listen precious, I've never gotten those pictures of my two kids you said you had had Robert Shaw make. Did you send them? Also take me some dolled up pictures of yourself. You seem to think precious that I dont want any more pictures of my big girl.

The ban (*sic*) of my life now sweetheart is that I have to stay dolled up in full regalia, my Sunday "go to meeting" clothes all the time. The Italian officers are great dressers and we have to be the same with them. It would amuse you to see me going out dyked up to kill with all my medals and decorations pinned to my puffed up manly chest and climbing up in a greasy oil sweating machine to fly that way. But it must be done for if you land in Germany you want your best clothes along to create the best possible impression.

I'm enclosing a post card picture of Daddy in his "old bus". I'm particularly proud of that picture and think I'll send one to each member of the family. So be sure and mention when you answer this letter that you have gotten the picture of Dad in his machine. Hear? Getting pretty conceited, aren't I? I almost forgot to tell you that Mr. Aswell was up here visiting our front and tried his best to find me but couldn't. I got a letter telling me of it after he had left. I was sorry not to have seen him. Now be two real good babies and kiss each other many times for Daddy. With all my love and a million kisses and hugs.

Your Devoted,
Paulie

O.K.
Paul M. Potts Jr.
1st Lieut A.S. Sig R.C.

17 Settembre 1918

Dearest Babykinses:-

In my letter yesterday I think I forgot to mention that I sent you another draft for $50.00 on the 4th of Sept. Be sure and mention it in your letters when you get it. Mr. Aswell told some of my flying comrades whom he met up on the front that he wanted to see me so as to tell you all about me and they said they had filled him full of bull. So I guess when he is next in Natchitoches he will give you lots of dope on me, that I haven't been able to write.

Dont you two kids let any one pass any wooden money off on you, and don't get too fat. Hear? For some reason or other this little cupie on this card reminds me of both of you.

With all my love and a million long kisses and hugs

Your Devoted
Paul.

19 Settembre 1918

Dearest Kids –

This gives you a hazy but nevertheless correct impression of the way it looks to "go over" on a bright moonlight night.

How are my two sweethearts today I wonder? I'm looking for those "dolled up" pictures awful hard now. I'm healthy well, and at least if not with (?) my ivory dome has good wearing qualities so dont worry. Saluti a bacci

Love Paulie.

Sept. 21, 1918.

Dearest Babykinses:-

Am leaving Italy for France. I may go on to England from there for a few months stay there. That's all the news I can impart. For a couple of months tho' you can rest easy again for I wont be flying in a war zone again for at least that long. So dont worry. Curt and I are going up together isn't that fine? Will write you volubly and love you lots when I get settled again. Be two good little kids like you always are and kiss each other a thousand times for Daddy. I'm well, contented and doing fine. All my love.

Your Paulie

Keep your mail coming to the same address in Italy and they will forward it to me.

❧ "POTTS, GO TO ENGLAND" ☙

American E. F.
Sept. 30th 1918

Dearest Babykins-

When you see that this is from England dont get alarmed and think I'm coming home – worse luck – this is about as near to home as I can expect to get for the "duration".

I had quite a pleasing trip up from my old station dear. All that kept it from being a perfect tour of Europe was because you two kids were not along. How I wished for you to enjoy it too. Curt K. and I had two days in "Gay Paree" and managed to get time to enjoy the frivolous city a little but didn't see or do anything noteworthy this trip.

I hated awfully to give up my old "bus". That, and bidding my Italian friends goodbye for what I expect is also the "duration" was the flaw in my happiness but "orders is orders". The colonel (Italian) who was our commander I used to tell you about came to the train with us to see us off so you see we left in quite a grand fashion. He had had a combination Italian-American flag made for our squadriglia to use.

Now I know you two cute kids are dying of curiosity, just like a couple of old maids, to know why and what for Daddy came to England. Well – but I'm not going to tell you – because I really dont know myself. The major writes to me in a telegram and says, says he, "Potts go to England" so here I am. And now

SEPTEMBER 30,
1918

219

that I'm here I suppose I'm to fly, since I'm labeled "aviator". But – I wont be flying the old "bus" I have been working on and liked so well but suppose it'll be something different. Anyway if it's a good bus I'm prepared to like it.

That marvelous picture of our young heiress (bless her heart) was delivered to me just before leaving and I alternated looking at it and the scenery all the way up and am afraid the scenery was neglected. You have been most outrageously deceiving me sweetheart, for except for her rosebud mouth she is the twin image of you. Shirley is just written all over her in box car letters and I'm more disappointed than ever that her name isn't Shirley too. I'm awful anxious to get the one of you together, but more of them later, for I've just arrived in London and must get thru my duties in time to rush around and see the place. Dont worry, for I'm fixed fine and in a very jolly state of mind. Being in Eng. is almost like being back in old U.S.A. Be good and kiss each other a thousand times for Daddy. With a million kisses and hugs and all my love

Your Devoted
Paulie.

Hold your mail for several days until you get my next letter giving new address.

O.K.
Paul M. Potts Jr.
1st Lieut. A.S. U.S.A.

American E. F.
Oct. 11, 1918.

My dearest Babykinses:-

I've been here about a week now and have received two letters from you dated Aug. 1 and 23, and two letters from Mama, dated Aug. 18 and 5. Your letter of the 23rd had that perfectly beautiful picture of my two kiddies in it and I've almost looked all the picture off it. I can't see dear where you all got the idea that our kiddy looks so much like me. Absolutely honey she is the image of you, and I'm ten times more proud of her since I've discovered it. Both of you are the sweetest best looking pair of girls in the whole world and that picture makes me awful awful homesick to get back to you.

I guess you see by the papers that the war is coming our way now so perhaps it wont be such an awful long time now before Daddy will get back to his kids.

OCTOBER 11, 1918

Being in England where I speak the "native language" and can read all the signs on the street corners is almost like being back in U.S.A. – almost but not quite! I had several very pleasant days in "old London" but didn't do any "site seeing". I have seen so darn many sights in the last year that I've lost interest in any new ones. Curt Keen and I did hire a cab and drive around some palace or other and the Parliament Buildings for 3½ shillings. Most of my days in London were spent at the Y.M.C.A. with my feet propped up before the first "fireplace with a fire in it" that I have seen for a year! By the way down here in camp we have real stoves and real coal, and most astonishing, we burn the coal in them and get warm. We are or rather I am fixed up very comfortably here and am getting fat as a pig on the eats I get. In London we saw a regular American show, Elsie Janis in "Hullo America". Enjoyed it imensely (*sic*), thought I'd swell up and burst with pride when she put on a Jazz Band act and then pulled her pockets wrong side out and they were made of two little American flags. Wonder why we Americans are all so darn proud of the fact that we are Americans??

All the afternoon I've been flying in the rain, and part of the time in a heavy blinding rain. The drops sting your face like needles until it smarts like everything. Once when I was coming down landing in the thickest blindingest rain of the afternoon with a film of water over my goggles so I couldn't read the blooming instruments in my machine, much less see the ground, a fellow driving a bunch of sheep scared me almost as bad as I scared him, for I could only see a dim green blur ahead that I took for our field and was diving down to it when all of a sudden a bunch of grey gyrating objects loomed up right in front of me and as I passed about four feet over them I recognized them to be the man and a bunch of sheep aforementioned. I fly here all the time I can get a machine in the air, just "stacking up hours" in the air, if you know what that means. And I'm flying one of the little stick control, tiny English machines that we Caproni pilots used to call "bugs" and "muskeeters" down In Italy. Why I don't know. But as long as Daddy is doing just this straight flying around here, and I will be for some time, you two kids dont have to worry about him coming home after the war for nothing ever happens to a fellow around here. It's so easy I hardly feel like I deserve my flying pay.

Just this note tonight dearest, for I'm very tired and it

takes all my spare time what little I get, to rest up. Anyway I want to look at that picture of you two kids some more, you pretty babies. Be real good and dont worry a bit for I'm alright and take good care of each other, hear? With a million long kisses and hugs and all my love

Your Daddy.

My address.
1st Lieut. Paul M. Potts Jr.
U.S. Air Service, A.E.F.
35 Eaton Place
London, S.W.I.
England.

A.E.F. OFFICERS' INN.
Oct. 22, 1918.
London, England

Dearest Babykinses:-

One of the things I've neglected to tell you before about my new camp is that I'm given one day a week to spend in London. That's why I'm here today, my "day off". It's awful nice for I come in and go to a show and forget all about flying for a whole day and get my nerves settled for another week of it.

I've gotten a number, about six, of your letters lately at camp but they all came from Italy. Of course I cant expect any from the new address yet tho'. The latest was dated about September 2 I think but I cant give you all the dates as I haven't them with me.

OCTOBER 22, 1918

The one with the little charm in it came and I was awful glad to get it. You dont understand precious that I knew I could have gotten them in Italy, every other shop window in Rome is full of them but it had to come from you for you are the person who charmed it for me. Capito?

Your Italian letter almost knocked me dead. Where do you get that stuff? I'll bet Mrs. Maggio corrected it, now didn't she? If she didn't then I'm perfectly scandalized to find I have an Italian speaking wife. I thought I knew my wife pretty well, but does she speak Italian? I find I've forgotten a great deal of the little I knew about it in just this short month I've been out of Italy. However if I ever go back there it will come back to me. You and I and nostra picola aviatrice (*sic*) will have to go there together some of these days.

There were two letters from Mother Potts and two from Mother Rollins that came last week. You'll have to forgive me for not writing more these days babykinses because I simply dont have the chance and the time. Every blessed day I spend on the flying field from 7 A.M. to 6 P.M. and when 6 P.M. comes naturally I'm ready for bed. The weather is great here, rains all the time, so you never have to bother with predicting the weather in the morning. You know it will be raining. However we fool the old weather man for we just go ahead and fly in the rain as if it wasn't raining. I'll write just every chance I get sweetheart but you'll know when you go a whole week without one that I simply didn't get a chance. Also dearest explain to the folks why I dont write them as much. I got the Kodak pictures of you two kids, honey, and honest you are both getting better looking all the time. Gracious but it makes me crazy to get back to you. You dont know sweetheart just how bad I do want to be with you again.

I'm glad Sis is with you all. She livens every thing up so and will keep you from "glooming" so much. I dont know whether to be glad or not that Billie has gone off to school. To me he's still just the same little boy and I cant imagine him as grown up and in long trousers. I'll try and write him if I can get the chance.

The clippings you sent me of letters from the home boys who are over here were very interesting but it seems queer to me to be reading those letters of former friends who have just come over when I've already been over a year now and gotten "aclimated" (*sic*) so to speak. The church in England which Adolph described, you know I saw from above last week, but didn't go in. Another fellow and I flew over it and circled around it when on a cross country flight. I've flown all over southern Eng. now on cross country trips.

You two kids be good now and dont worry a bit about Daddy for now since I have your little charm I'm doubly safe. I'll write as often as I can sweetheart. Kiss each other a thousand times for Dad and love him lots. With a million long kisses and hugs and all my love

Your Devoted
Paulie.

O.K.
Paul M. Potts Jr.
1st Lieut. A.S. U.S.A.

OVERDOSE OF HEAVY NIGHT BOMBING

American Exp. F.
England, Oct. 26, 1918

Dearest Babykinses:-

Today I received your sweet letters of Sept. 11, 12 and 15 and yesterday I received those of the 5 and 17. Also I got Dad's of Sept. 2 and Mother Rollins' of the 16. One of yours had that precious cap in it and the other the print of our rascal's foot. I wouldn't take any thing for either one dearest, you dont know how priceless they are to me. It was awful sweet of you to think of sending them. Now, who says I haven't the best little wife in the world? I hadn't realized before really, how small that youngster was.

My card numbering ran out dearest because I heard from supposedly good authority that picture post cards were disapproved by the censors and I haven't sent you any cards since leaving Italy because I understand it's against regulations up here. I'll find out for sure as soon as I can.

OCTOBER 26, 1918

You know that fussy letter I wrote from Ghedi wasn't intended to be so terribly fussy honey, but I guess it was pretty bad. You know you had been writing me some awful gloomy letters and that coupled with the fact that my nerves were on a raw edge from an overdose of flying made me make it look worse than it really was. But since then sweetness your letters have been just gems of cheerfulness and courage. Good, cheerful, letters from you change my mental attitude entirely and I can always fly more cheerfully and with a better judgement it seems after getting a bunch. But we'll forget that letter of mine and kiss and make up. Haven't you found out yet sweetheart that the main reason I ever fuss with you is to get to kiss and make up afterward? It's so nice!

Just as I was getting all settled to spend a good part of the winter here dearest, I suddenly changed my mind and decided to sojourn a while in France. Also a piece of good news, I dont think I'm going to have to do any more night flying. Think I'm scheduled for day work only over there. I hope so. Dont get flurried now precious for I'm not going to the front again just yet. Only to another flying center. I hope to get to the front again sweetheart before it's over, in a light combat machine and a heavy night bombing pilot hasn't a chance of getting a Hun, except on the ground with his bombs and I dont like 'em that way.

I'm enclosing a "Christmas Coupon" but dont know whether it will reach you in time for you to get the package off before Nov. 20th as it requires or not. If not it doesn't matter sweetheart for I have all I need but if it reaches you in time then please make the contents: 3 pkgs of Colgates (*sic*) Toothpaste, 8 cans of Prince Albert pipe tobacco and the rest in prauleins? (*sic*), you know the pecan candy like you sent last Xmas if you have the pecans and the sugar (if u haven't any sugar just stir them up with yours and P's finger. C?) and Pauline will let you make it. Use my English address until you get my French one.

Be two very good babies now and kiss each other a
thousand times for Daddy. Will write again as soon as possible.
With a million long kisses and hugs and all my love

Your Devoted
Paulie.

O.K.
Paul M. Potts Jr.
1st Lieut. Air Service.

—

A.E.F. England.
Nov. 1, 1918

Dearest Babykinses:-

Just another of my short notes. I expect some of these days you are going to haul off and tell me you want a letter and not just a short note. I was in London yesterday and so sent you a draft for $500.00 thru the American Express Co. there. They said it ought to reach you in three weeks. Think you get a draft or check from the office at Natch. when it gets there. It's more or less yours and Pauline's Xmas present, and now dont go put it all in the bank and refuse to spend any of it. C? Dont worry about me for I'm keeping a reserve fund of $250.00 with me. I've been awful

November 1, 1918

tickled and relieved too since I got your letter telling me you had a good nurse to help you with Pauline. You simply must keep her sweetheart if for nothing more than my feelings. I got a "strayed" letter from you this morn dated June 29th, but it was sweet even if it was four months old. I also got one from Cousin Mary Haynes dated Sept 20 and she said she was making Pauline some "things". May I answer her letter???

When I go back over to France I'm going to leave a suit case full of "junk" stored with the American Exp. Co.

in London. The "junk" is just discarded odds and ends that I dont use any more but hate to throw away but the real object is that since I lost my duffle bag with about $100.00 worth of shoes, clothes, flying equipment etc. on the journey up from Italy, most of which I had to replace when I got here, I want to leave my Kodak book with it's year's collection of Italian pictures in safe keeping and so that is really the only valuable in it. It (my Kodak book) was almost ruined by that monkey "Lulu" whom I used to write you about, during my last days in Italy. He slipped into my room one day and turned the oil lamp over on my table and the oil just soaked thru and thru my Kodak book. The pictures are pretty greasy but only a few are blurred by it. However that wasn't all he did. He tore up a bunch of official papers, took a bottle of iodine off my dresser and just poured it all over my toilet articles, clothes and bed. If I had caught him at it I'd have choked him to death even if he was a colonel's pet monkey and I was only a 1st Lieut. I got my orderly and we went out to look for him with a pair of clubs but he couldn't be found. However that night when he wandered in the colonel gave him a good beating, to my entire satisfaction. So you see my Kodak book has a history.

I'm enclosing a rather ridiculous looking picture. You know I wrote you before that the Italian colonel who commanded the camp said he had a menagerie of 2 dogs, 2 monkeys and 7 Americans. Well there's the seven of us the day before we left. I was the C.O. of the group dont it look it? The darn picture makes us all look like a bunch of reprobates and toughs but when we all got dressed up we were not so bad (looking) and they were certainly a nice bunch of fellows.

Give love to Sis and Elizabeth and you two babies kiss each other a thousand times for Daddy and be two real good

kids till I come home. (Which ought not to be so far off according to the "War News") Think so??
      With a million kisses and hugs and all my love

Your Devoted
Paulie.

O.K.
Paul M. Potts Jr.
1st Lieut. Air Service

American Washington Inn for Officers
YMCA St. James's Square
London, S.W. 1.
England
Nov. 3rd, 1918.

Dearest Babykinses:-

This is a bally glooming day in London, meaning to say that it's raining as usual. I hope the weather over in France is not like this! By the way dearest when you get this I'll probably be back over there, much to my satisfaction, although I've thoroughly enjoyed this sojourn in England. It's been a real treat, being back in a country where I speak the language. I've seen all the best shows in London too which has been another treat. You know after the war I think I'll become a "traveling man" for since I left old Foggia I haven't stayed in any place longer than a month! What do you think of it. I've had lots of experience now. But I know you two kids wont stand for being left at home any more than I'd leave you.

NOVEMBER 3, 1918

Listen dear, in one of your late letters you mentioned getting the piccola or piceola? (*sic*) aviatrice a violin from Italy. I wish I had thought of it in Foggia for we had two celebrated concert violinists there in my camp and I could have gotten them to go with me to help me choose a good one. Both of them had a perfect craze for wandering through the music

233

shops of Rome. However I dont know if I could have sent it home. We'll get her a make shift to use until we visit Rome in 19??. "C"?

Do you remember the day I took you out to Training Camp in Little Rock and Albert W., Marion H. and a fellow named Sam Long who joked so about his girls came out to the car? Well he was in a camp not far from my aerodrome a few weeks back and I almost saw him! A boy named Griffin who was in my company in T.C. and came into aviation just after me was down at my field and while flying a cross country trip had a forced landing near the camp and was taken in there. The stuff Long told him to tell me would fill a book, especially the part he said for me to write you. I flew over the place a few days later intending to land and see him but there wasn't a decent field to come down within two miles of the place so I had to come back.

You know I haven't seen a soul whom I knew before the war for over a year now? Curt Keen and McCain, possibly you remember him, and Griffin are the only fellows I've seen out of my ground school for six months! By the way you remember the ten fellows I started out of ground school with? Well only one, Mason, perhaps you remember him, has been killed so far and the rest are scattered over Eng., France and Italy. Stone and Adriance, you remember them, have quit flying long ago and are on ground jobs. Both of them had rather serious "crashes" down at Foggia so I dont blame them.

I dont know why I'm telling you all this "family history" today unless it's because I haven't anything else to write, but I know you like to hear about the bunch I came over with. What I'd like to write about is my two kids, especially the biggest one, tho' she's not very big at that, (not quite one "armful") but she has the most beautiful brown hair and eyes and a "turn up" nose, very pretty in fact. She used to have a dimple too, but I dont know if she still has it. I have quite an affinity for her, like her very much in fact. The smallest one

I dont know much about except on "hear say" but she is the image of the biggest one, which is what I like most about her and that also makes me like her very much.

I guess I better mention again sweetheart that I sent you a draft for $500.00 on the 1st of Nov. through the American Express Co. here. Notify me soon as you get it. Guess I must stop 'till next time now tho' I dont want to.

Be two very good kiddies now and kiss each other lots for Daddy. With all my love and a million kisses and hugs

Your Devoted
Paulie.

O.K.
Paul M. Potts Jr.
1st Lieut. Air Service.

——

§ SLIPPERS & DUNHILL PIPE ¢

AMERICAN YMCA
Washington Inn for Officers
St. James's Square
London, S.W. 1., England
Nov. 5, 1918

Dearest Babykinses:-

Today I sent you and mother a pair of slippers each and Dad a pipe. To save me I couldn't remember the size foot you possess so got them the size I think your foot or rather feet used to look. But remember sweetheart its been a year since I've seen those feet so dont blame me too much if they are rather large. I haven't any idea that you or mother either one will be able to wear them but the intentions were good, weren't they? I tried to find something for the kiddie but dearest I'm an awful inefficient Daddy for to save me I cant think of any thing a young lady like that would like to have.

Tell Dad his pipe is a "Dunhill" from London. Said to be made out of briar over 100 yrs. old. I got myself one and was so tickled with it that I couldn't resist sending him one also. If you were an old pipe smoker I'd send you one too!

I must thank you for that kind permission to write to Cousin Mary. No, But really sweetheart, she wrote me two very nice letters and told me all about my kids so I thought perhaps you'd want me to.

NOVEMBER 5, 1918

I am just about to make this a letter dearest instead of the short note but my times up again. Be two dear sweet babies like you have so long and kiss each other a thousand times for Daddy. With a million kisses and hugs and all my love.

Your Devoted
Paulie.

O.K.
Paul M. Potts Jr.
1st Lieut. Air Service

❧ OFFICERS' REST HOUSE IN FRANCE ❧

E.F.C.
OFFICERS REST HOUSE AND MESS
A.E.F. France
Nov. 8th 1918

Dearest Babykinses-

Well here I am back in France, and of course well pleased and contented as usual. I couldn't resist the temptation to write to you on this paper so you can see I'm in a rest house and mess. There's no rest for the weary tho' is there?

The war news or rather the peace news is so good now that I'm about ready to pack up and come home. Any way you two kids had better get your dimples ready to work in the next six months or so.

I had thought I was going to be back in the "Gay Paree" today but as you can see by the paper I'm not, but "resting" instead, and taking this opportunity to give you kids a line so you wont be worrying about Daddy. Be real good and kiss each other a thousand times for me. With all my love and a million kisses and hugs

Your Devoted
Paulie.

O.K.
Paul M. Potts Jr.
1st Lieut. Air Service

NOVEMBER 8, 1918

ARMISTICE CELEBRATED
IN FRANCE

HOTEL NEGRESCO
37 PROMENDE des. ANGLAIS
NICE
Nov. 16th, 1918

My darling Babykinses

Le guerre est fini! But not quite for Daddy I'm sorry to say. Monday when the news came that the armistice had been signed all my old bunch of Caproni drivers were ready to say, "No more flying for me". Especially me! But the Colonel (I was at the 3rd A. I. C. France) called us over and explained why we had to go right on flying just as hard as before until the peace documents are all signed and old Uncle Sammy says we can go home and quit. He has spent thousands and thousands of dollars on us already and now we've got to stay with him until he dont need us any longer. Why I venture to say my training expenses alone together with the Capronis (*sic*) I've smashed up have cost in the neighborhood of $50,000. So you see dearest although my duties to you two kids require that I take no more chances and come home to you safe, I've just got to go right on taking my same chances for a few more months, to justify my training.

NOVEMBER 16, 1918

I know you were overjoyed when you heard that the war was over and I dont want to damp a bit of that joy so I'm promising to fly high and fast which is safest and not low and slow and to think of you two kids all the time so I can come back to you in a few months.

I'm taking the first regular seven days leave I've had since I've been over here, with another Caproni pilot named Earnest Whittemore. We got our leave the day the armistice was signed and were in Paris the day after for the tremendous celebration there. I'll tell you all about it later for it was some celebration. I'm down here at Nice and will take up the rest of my time here and at Monte Carlo. I've already been over there one day and seen the Cassino (*sic*) where all the famous gambling goes on, but we are not allowed in the place during gambling hours so I didn't actually see them playing. It was very interesting. Monte Carlo is a regular little doll house of a place. Absolutely the most beautiful and expensive place I ever have seen. I like Nice very much too. It's very nice. When I arrived at my new station in France I found three sweet letters from you waiting for me. One had that little crucifix, or whatever you call it with the little medal on it and another had two more sweet pictures of our kiddy. She's growing awfully fast sweetheart and in every picture you send me she looks more like her beautiful mother. I still have to fuss tho' honey because you wont send me pictures of my big baby too. I simply must have pictures of you sweetheart every time you send pictures of the little girl. Now dont neglect Daddy that way any more.

However precious I expect that we'll be together again before many more moons and you wont have so very much time to send me pictures before I'll see you two precious in the original. Do you realize sweetheart that right up to date it has been fifteen months since I've seen you. If I dont see you in another three months I think I'm going to just collapse like a rubber balloon stuck with a pin. I feel sure tho' sweetheart that I'll at least be on the way to see you in that time. I think we can count on it. When I do get there, us two and the kiddie must have a honeymoon for a couple of weeks where we wont have to bother about anybody but ourselves. Do you want to?

Yesterday a business man here took us out to his home for lunch. Whittemore had a letter of introduction to him from a firm in the states. He is an olive oil dealer and refiner and is a millionaire as millionaires go over here. But best of all he and his family are pure Italians. So he gave us an out and out Italian family lunch from Macaroni and red wine on down to fruit and coffee. All his family except his wife spoke good English, having traveled in America, and after lunch his daughter, a little girl of about ten played all the latest American Rags for us. It's one of the most interesting things that has happened to me. He also took us through his oil refinery and explained his whole business. His offices we found fitted up more like rest rooms than work rooms.

Well sweetheart, dont forget for one single instant that I'll be thinking of you all the time until I come home again and be good both of you kids and kiss each other a thousand times for Daddy. With a million kisses and hugs and all my love

Your devoted
Paulie

Address-
Paul M. Potts, Jr. 1st Lt. A.S.
3rd A. I. C. Issoudon, France
American Exp. F.

HOTEL NEGRESCO
37 Promenade des Anglais.
NICE
Nov. 20, 1918

Dearest Babykinses:-

I've had an awful pleasant stay down here in spite of the fact that I feel like I shouldn't spend the money a vacation like this requires since the war is over. But you know sweetheart they wanted me to start flying those bally little Nieuports and since I had the privilege of this leave first if I wanted it I couldn't resist taking this extra time to think it over. When I finish up the required course of flying on them I dont see why they shouldn't begin to figure on when they will send me back home to you two kids do you? That's all I can think of now, the time when I'll get back to you.

Listen sweetheart the address I left my Kodak book at in London, was the American Exp. Co. 6 Haymarket St. London, S. W. I stored it in a suitcase you know and just give you the address, so in case you should want it and didn't bring it home, you could get it, Capito? Wonder if you got those $500 "bucks" thru' the Am. Exp. Co. there O.K. and also those slippers?

I'm rather anxious to get back to Issoudon to see how much mail has accumulated there for me from my babykins as well as to get my foot in one of those Nieuports and put in the

November 20,
1918

required number of hours in them and get thru with it.

The weather down here is almost as pleasant as in Italy at this time of the year and it's going to be "bad news" for me to have to wade back into the knee deep mud of Issoudon and go to sleeping in a rough sleeping bag on a canvas bunk after a week of this luxurious life. However sweetheart I can go to it with a fairly good will now since I can see or think I can see an end in future to this rough life away from you. I really think you will be getting more "dope" on the probable time us fellows will be allowed to return to home and civil life than I'm getting over here, for all that any one over here seems to know about it is that we'll "carry on", as the English say, just as we were doing before the armistice. I've heard speculations on my length of time from those months to a year and a half, as the time before we'll get home so I can't say how much longer it may be before we'll get together again. At any rate sweetheart you want to begin getting "fat" (not too fat) and get that dimple ready for business now at most any time.

I know you wonder why I dont tell you more about Nice and Monte Carlo but sweetness it seems I've been over here so long now that I dont know how to tell you about the sights in these places. They've actually gotten so they seem perfectly natural and ordinary whereas the strangeness of New York would cause me to "gush".

Be two real, real good little kids now and kiss each other many times for Daddy. With a million kisses and hugs and all my love

Your Devoted
Paulie.

Address.
Paul M. Potts Jr. 1st Lieut. A.E.
3rd A. I. C. Issoudon France
American Exp. F.

Dec. 2nd 1918

Dearest Babykinses:-

I know you two kids have been wondering what has become of all Daddy's letters lately and I'll tell you I've been so busy and anxious figuring out how to get ordered home to you that I've been putting off writing every day saying "Wait till tomorrow and maybe I'll be able to tell them I'm coming home". But I cant tell yet. However, I believe Christmas day will find me on the way across the ocean. So you kids had better look out. If you're both not fat and slick as a pair of kittens with all your dimples out and working – Oh what I wont do to you! I'm not flying any more over here so I'm in no more danger and you kids can sit down to Christmas dinner knowing that Daddy is just as safe as you are. Today is my birthday and I'm very happy because I know I'll be home to celebrate both my kids birthdays. With all my love and a million kisses and hugs,

your, Paulie.

DECEMBER 2, 1918

❧ SIMPLY PLAYED OUT ❧

A.E.F. France
Dec. 7, 1918

My darling Babykinses:-

Just got four letters from you yesterday afternoon, No. 7 dated Sept 23, No. 11, dated Sept. 29, No. 13, dated Oct. 3, and No. 21, dated Nov. 6. Hows (*sic*) that for a nice complete bundle of mail. If it was a month ago I'd be mad as thunder at the P.O. for losing all those in between but now it doesn't make so much difference for in a couple of months at least I'm going to be with you and this letter business will be a thing of the past for good.

I've done just about everything possible to get ordered home dearest and am impatiently waiting results. It will probably be two more weeks before I'll know whether I'm going to get home right away or have to stay over here. It seems to be the dope that they want the men who have been over here longest to stay over here except a few lucky ones.

I'm doing my level best to be one of the lucky ones and if I succeed I hope they will give me my discharge papers when I hit New York and let me go home "free" to my kids. Not that I dislike the Army or any thing like that, for it's the best and greatest old army in the world, but I'm simply played out and am no more good until I get back to you kids and get some "pep". I haven't any heart left for anything over here. The prospects of going up with the Occupation Army and flying

DECEMBER 7, 1918

around Germany holds no interest for me. If I had you kids over here it would be fine. Just to boil it down to hard facts I guess that I've just been away from you for so long now that I'm deathly homesick for you. As I told you I'm done flying over here. I dont have to take another flight, so you can rest easy about my being "bumped off" in an accident. Unless the boat hits a rock going home I'm going to get there sure.

I'm glad you finally opened up and told me all about Billie boy, for up until today I've been completely in the dark about him. Next summer you and I can keep him around us most of the time perhaps and then I can get back my old influence over him and establish him on the right tract. I tell you a boys associates at his age have a lot to do with his life and character.

Listen sweetheart, I hope you went on and visited Mary and insisted on taking your nurse with you. In my eyes, the most pitiful and "tacky" sight I know is a young wife traveling alone with a baby on one arm and a suit case on the other. I dont want any wife of mine doing it! "C?" So if the folks argued you out of taking nurse then I hope you stayed home! Sis always had her nurse with her when she came home with Elizabeth and so I cant see why the folks should object to you taking one too. Capito?

I wish you all had been keeping me posted on such things as Mama's health and operation. Knowing all about such things doesn't worry me near as much as just having a hint here and there with no information. Now I will be worried about Mama until I get home and see her for myself.

Influenza has been raging over here as it has over there and I've been worried for fear you all would have it. Over in England it was pretty fatal. Now, I understand if a fellow has it, they send him home as soon as he is able to be about so I wouldn't mind at all having it. However there's still pretty good prospects of my getting started home before Xmas so "cheerio" as the English say.

—

Be two real good kids now and polish up those dimples for they aren't going to ring me in on any of that 18 months more foreign service stuff. I'm going to be with you before summer or in an army "bug house".

With a million hugs and kisses and all my love

Your Devoted
Paulie.

I've been wondering who was going to have to occupy that "Kiddie Coop" when I get home. Me or Pauline?

S.O.A. meaning "Same Old Address".

❦ NO KIND OF LIFE ❦

3rd A.I.C., A.E.F
France, Dec. 23, 1918

My darling Babykinses:-

Well here it is the day before Christmas Eve and it just happened to occur to me. Three weeks ago it really looked like I was going to be lucky dearest and would be on my way home by Christmas day but my luck must have changed for I'm still here at 3rd A.I.C. and dont know when I'll get away. But I'll tell you this much sweetheart, I do really believe that with no very bad luck I'll get started home before the last of March. Of course I'm not doing anything, just stagnating but I understand the home going boats are crowded and we have to wait our turn. Any way sweetheart it will be nicer to get home to you two kids in the warm spring than in the winter, eh?

You know I've completely made up my mind that I wont stay in the army in peace time. It's no kind of life for a married man. Here I've been in it a year and eight months and haven't seen you for a year and four months. Yes sir, I'm going to be a civilian and live with my wife and kiddie just as soon as I can. Now that brings up the question of what shall we do? I was counting on us three kids getting out on the plantation until Dad disposed of it. There's nothing I'd rather do than live in the country on a small farm with just us. But I suppose

DECEMBER 23,
1918

next fall we shall have to become the Mr. and Mrs. Proffessor. At any rate we'd better wait until I get home to bother about that.

I scarcely ever get any more letters from you honey. I know you write them and it makes me awful mad to know that they are lying up on some dusty P.O. shelf somewhere. The last I got you were in Monroe and I was awful relieved to have you say you had taken nurse with you for I'd have hated awful bad for you to be traveling around trying to carry an armful of babies and suit cases all by yourself.

It absolutely rains, rains every day here. It's raining now, was raining yesterday and last week and will be raining tomorrow and next week. However the mud is only up to your knees and never cakes on you more than half an inch thick. I was very curious to find out who it was that called France, "Sunny France". Well the other day a Y.M.C.A. lecturer told me. The term, "Sunny France" was first used by an Englishman and England is the only country in the world where the sun shines less than it does in France. I understand that there are old grey headed people in England who never having been fortunate enough to travel out of the country have never seen the sun except behind fog and clouds. Can you beat it?

I guess you can tell by this letter how full of the Christmas spirit I am and how much I'm enjoying my sojourn in France.

I'll be thinking of my two kiddies every minute and longing to get back to them harder than ever before, and hopeing (*sic*) Christmas is more like Christmas to you two babies. Love to all the folks and with a million long kisses and hugs and all my love to you. Kiss each other lots and lots for Daddy

Your Devoted
Paulie.

Dont forget to be working on those dimples and getting

them ready, for if you're not as fat and plump as I told you to
be, look out.

O.K.
Paul M. Potts Jr.
1st Lt, Air Service

HOTEL CONTINENTAL
3 Rue Castiglione
Paris
Jan. 1st 1919

My darling Babykinses-

Happy New Year to you two kids! I'm passing thru Paris for the last time I hope sweetheart as I'm on my way to a port to be sent home! I've just cabled you to stop writing and I know you'll be looking for me to show up just about the time my cable reaches you. You sweet thing! But I do hope to be with you two babies in another two months, that is the latter part of Feb. And I hope to be a free man, not belonging to anybodies army when I do reach you again. I've had enough of war and army life to last me the rest of my natural life.

JANUARY 1, 1919

Of course darling I'll have to wait a couple of weeks or so for a boat when I get to the port tomorrow and then it will probably take me as long or longer to get released from the army when I reach New York. But cheer up and get those precious brown eyes and dimples in order for I'll surely be home before the end of Feb. Want me much?? As I want you????

I want to see you two babies so, so bad darling and to collect some of those millions of long kisses that you, my "biggest baby" have been saving up for me for so long now and to squeeze you tight once again so hard darling that it's an

awful temptation not to ask you to meet me in New York. But
it would be an awful trying trip on you two babies as well as
expensive so I guess it's really best for you to wait for Daddy
to get home to you. It'll only be a couple of weeks longer at
the most. So be two real, real good girlies as you've been for
Daddy for so long now and you my "big baby" dont forget
those brown eyes, dimples and tulips. With a million long long
kisses and all my love

Your Devoted
Paulie.

  Hope old man Censor enjoys this! But remember if you're
not at least as "fat" as you were in Austin something terrible
will be coming to you. *P*

———

252

EPILOGUE

&

AFTER WORLD WAR I, Paul Potts resigned his commission and went to Houston, Texas to work for The Texas Company. His wife, Shirley, and daughter Pauline (later known as Paula) went with him. When Mother Potts died, Paul's father decided to sell everything and move to Shreveport, Louisiana. So my father bought the "Green House" back in Natchitoches, along with the portion of his father's land which was suitable for raising cotton and other crops, which my family called "the place." Families who lived on "the place" tended the crops and the daily chores, and my father and mother settled down to raise their family in the Green House in town. (Evidently my mother was not interested in living on "the place," perhaps because her family was growing, and there were schools to consider for the children, and friends for them to play with closer to town.)

1) First daughter Paula did get her violin. And she graduated with a double major in piano and violin from Newcomb College in New Orleans.

2) Paul and Shirley had a second daughter and named her Shirley. Are you surprised? She married a World War II pilot who flew the English Spitfire fighter plane. After the war, Shirley and her husband, who was by then an Air Attaché, went to Baghdad and later, Burma.

3) My brother, Paul Mimms Potts, III, was the son they hoped for. He died at the age of 12 from a tragic accident at a Boy Scout gathering. Two boys, roughhousing, fell on him as he lay, relaxed, perhaps gazing at the constellations. This

———

ruptured his spleen and he died on the operating table. It was terribly sad and traumatic for everyone. My father hid his grief and remained strong for us all, just as the story in his letters where he said "You just grin and bear it". But he didn't grin, for I'm sure it just broke his heart.

4) As for me, I taught Speech and Drama in a small girls' college in New Orleans. I was 20. A friend helped me earn 9 hours flying time in his own plane; my final feat was mapping out my own route from New Orleans to Baton Rouge. At home, as I related what I had done, my mother and father did not react at all. Later, she said they hoped I would lose interest – and I did. Had they objected or shared my father's wartime experiences, I might have kept on! Remember, as the young one in the family, I never knew my father had ever been in an airplane. Now, because of these letters, I know.

5) Do you also remember my father's sister, the lively one, who came home from Texas with her baby? Well, that baby grew up and joined the Women's Air Force Service, the WAFS, and flew the early DC3s ferrying equipment and supplies across the Atlantic during World War II.

6) As far as I know, my father never took my mother up in an airplane, but maybe he did before I was born. He never mentioned the War or VMI or flying. As far as keeping in touch with anyone, the only one I know of was Curt Keen who came to visit. I never heard such talk and laughter and never saw my father and mother as jolly as on that visit. I paid no attention to what they were saying. I just know it made my father very happy. I know that. My parents never went to Europe together, either. There was a Depression and then World War II, and the deaths in my family of Mother Rollins, Mother Potts, my grandfather Potts and my brother Paul, all conspired to alter my father's plans and dreams.

7) There was the fire in 1932. It rarely snows in Louisiana, so when a freak storm hit the area that winter, the seven fireplaces in the old wooden Green House had burned most

of the day. The fires had been stoked by Zeke, the house boy. With only Mother Rollins and my father at home, asleep, the fire started and then raged through the house: my grandmother and father just barely escaped with their lives. My father stood, in pajamas, barefooted in the snow on a burlap bag, and watched his house burn to the ground. Everything was lost, but somehow I have these few pictures and letters. (They must have been kept at another location, for they never would have survived the fire.) The family built another house on the same property, which was right at the entrance of the college in Natchitoches.

8) My father died in 1953 at age 57. He was very ill with Hodgkin's disease before he died. My mother lived 19 more years without him.

9) Remember my mother said to me, "Here are Paul's letters. I want you to have them", and I had not read them for 40 years? Last fall my husband made me read them to him. I said, "But they are so fragile. They are nearly 100 years old and besides, they are private." His answer was, "Well, don't listen. Just read." I did, and he has had me read them many times since. After hearing me read them he said, "I wish I had known him. I would have liked him." That pleases me.

10) When I was in my late teens, almost 20, I thought my parents were old in their mid-50's. In my apparent arrogance, I felt I should impart my infinite wisdom to them. (On reflection, I was infinitely ignorant.) I thought I had discovered Shakespeare – but our old family "bible", passed down with genealogical data, was actually a leatherbound gold-trimmed Shakespearean volume, to be passed on to the men of the Potts family. I now have that book, though it's very worn and tattered. Go figure!

NOTES

☙

Note, Introduction, page 10:

Arriving in France with other volunteers, they ran into Major Fiorello LaGuardia, who was in charge of the new Air Service flight training center in Foggia, Italy. This was the same man who was to become Mayor of New York City and the namesake of LaGuardia Airport.

LaGuardia selfishly arranged orders so that the misrouted Cadets were sent to his own school at Foggia. There, the instructors were mostly Italian, so the orphaned group dropped their French dictionaries and quickly picked up Italian ones. The training aircraft were French-built Farmans and three large, cumbersome Italian Capronis.

The first group of 47 flight candidates arrived in France in late June 1917, but the bulk of trainees did not arrive until fall, missing the best training time and crowding the French and embryonic U.S. training facilities in France.

A first detachment of 46 U.S. cadets arrived at the Italian flight school at Foggia on 28 September, to be joined by another detachment in October that included first-term congressman from New York Fiorello H. LaGuardia.

Excerpted from: Morrow, John H., Jr. *The Great War in the Air: Military Aviation from 1909 to 1921.* Washington, DC. Smithsonian History of Aviation Series. 1993.

Note, "A WILD-EYED RIDE", page 134

Another of the new pilots to be evaluated was Percy W. "Red" Graham, a redheaded Chicago native and one of that city's most celebrated collegiate athletes. He was a pole-vault champion, a sprinter, a hurdler, and a star football quarterback at the University of Chicago before he volunteered for the Air Service.

Excerpted from: Woolley, Charles with Bill Crawford. *Echoes of Eagles: A Son's Search for His Father and the Legacy of America's First Fighter Pilots*. New York: New American Library, 2004.

Note, NERVOUS AS THUNDER, page 155

I have read a number of books since discovering my fathers' letters, and I would have wished to include many excerpts, but space and time does not allow me to reproduce all the interesting details I have discovered. Yet, this one excerpt (*below*) matches the letters about night flying stress my father tells about as he is being called to do night flying more and more. A pilot must lose a lot of sleep as it plays on his nerves. *Ed.*

...in 1916, began a gradual conversion to night bombing by all the belligerents on the Western Front.

On the Italian front some daylight bombing also persisted, though there was a move to convert long distance operations to nighttime – notably the bombing 'duel' the belligerents carried on back and forth across the Adriatic, the Austrians attacking port facilities at Venice, and the Italians bombing the Austrian naval base at Pola.

Training bomber crews for night operations was challenging work, which cost much in fatigue and also unfortunately lives sacrificed." Some airmen who were excellent pilots in the daytime remained totally disoriented at night; for the first time the problem of nightblindness manifested itself. Night flying required navigational skills not required by day. In some units the flying was done when there was sufficient moonlight or starlight to make out something of the terrain below—perhaps one night in three. But as the war progressed the night flyers acquired considerable skill in navigating by the stars or by compass.

If we are to believe those who participated in them,

night bombing missions were never humdrum affairs. Franz Schlenstedt recalled that a nighttime takeoff in a heavily laden bomber from a field that was usually too short 'was, God knows, no easy matter.' Once aloft, there were other risks. There were the enemy's guns and searchlights of course, but there was also the risk of mechanical breakdown. In the daytime a pilot worried about engine failure only when he was on the enemy side of the line; at night he had to worry about it all the time, for a 'blind' emergency landing at night often ended in catastrophe. The final task was to find one's own flare-lit airfield or, barring that, one of the emergency fields.

Excerpted from: Kennett, Lee, *The First Air War: 1914–1918*. New York, New York: The Free Press, 2001

Night flying was being explored and developed as a tool of war sometime around 1916. Paul's letters describe many of its difficulties. He states in one letter as he is about to fly at night, "I'm nervous as thunder". It's no wonder! Pilots who excelled at flying in the daytime didn't always adjust well to night flying. First, a flyer's internal clock for sleep is disturbed and the constant stress causes much fatigue. Taking off in planes – with an additional load of bombs, on short runways, in the night, headed to unfamiliar destinations, guided only by the constellations and possibly a compass – is very challenging, but there is that additional disorientation and night blindness condition that must be compensated for. Then, having averted detection, and after dropping the load of bombs, the pilot must find the way back to his field, or an emergency field if necessary, and land with only flares lighting the runway. I think it was an daunting task in that day and age of flying experimentation. *Ed.*

Note, Letter transcription, pages 208–211:

Dear Kids: Here's Potts and Ragnelli interrupted in a deep conversation to have their pictures taken. They are two famous bombing pilots. Bet Bill Kaiser would give a lot to know what these two guys were plotting

Here's the "gang." Zannini is entertaining.

Some of the powers that were in my former squadron.

This is the way the ground looks from 6000 ft. Curt Keen was driving while I took this picture. The film was splotched some.

The famous headless statue of Rome.

Ragnelli caught treating to chocolate. In back ground is Minardis the sergeant who flew with me down to the new camp and landed our bus in the cow pasture.

Pica and Vertus, the mascot.

That's me! Keen caught me coming from this little church one Sunday morn and took my picture in the act. "The camera's eye don't lie."

More Pica and Vertus with the action on the Vertus.

A glimpse of the famous old Tiber River where it flows through Rome.

Entrance to the king's palace in Rome.

Fragmentary glimpses of "my old bus" which I'm hoping the Censor will pass but am afraid he wont.

With a million kisses to you both and all my love, be good, Your devoted... That's me!

FURTHER READING

Kennett, Lee. *The First Air War: 1914–1918*. New York: The Free Press. 1991.

Morrow, John H., Jr. *The Great War in the Air: Military Aviation from 1909 to 1921*. Washington, DC. Smithsonian History of Aviation Series. 1993.

Woolley, Charles with Bill Crawford. *Echoes of Eagles: A Son's Search for His Father and the Legacy of America's First Fighter Pilots*. New York: New American Library, 2004.

ABOUT THE EDITOR

MARION POTTS CLAYTON is the only living child of Paul and Shirley Potts, the former the writer of the letters and the latter the bride receiving the letters. Marion was born in Natchitoches, Louisiana, in the "Green House," the name given to the family home of her father and grandfather. She fondly remembers her young years in Natchitoches. The town was founded in 1714 by Louis Juchereau de St. Denis. Its name

Marion Potts Clayton

is derived from a Native American tribe, and it is noted as being the oldest town in the Louisiana Purchase.

Marion moved to Yorktown, Virginia with her husband, Howard, in 1988. Her home and neighbors within this village are surrounded by the National Historic Battlefield Park, the place where General George Washington defeated British General Cornwallis in the last major battle of the Revolution in 1781. Her main interest, outside of her father's letters and her family, is her membership in the Comte de Grasse Chapter, Daughters of the American Revolution (DAR). She was honored to become their Regent in 2004–2007 and soon afterward learned that her mother Shirley, Paul's wife, had been the Founding Regent of the St. Denis DAR Chapter in Natchitoches. Her mother, sister Pauline, and grandmother ("Mother Rollins") had all been DAR members. She finds this ironic: not only had she not known that her father was an aviator in World War I (since he never spoke of the war or aviation), but she also had been unaware that her mother was a DAR Regent, and a Founding Regent at that!

Marion and Howard Clayton have a son, John, (and daughter-in-law, Michelle) and a daughter, Sarah, (and son-in-law, Bruce) as well as three grandchildren: Clayton (and wife, Laura), Caroline and William.